A WOMAN'S PLACE .... ?

A Woman's Place .... ?

Women and Work

Edited by
ELIZABETH TEMPLETON

SAINT ANDREW PRESS
EDINBURGH

First published in 1993 by
SAINT ANDREW PRESS
121 George Street, Edinburgh EH2 4YN
on behalf of
SCOTTISH CHURCHES' INDUSTRIAL MISSION

Copyright © Scottish Churches' Industrial Mission 1993

ISBN 0 86153 162 0

British Library Cataloguing in Publication Data
    A catalogue record for this book
    is available from The British Library

    ISBN 0-86153-162-0

This book is set in 10.5/12 pt Times Roman.

Printed and bound in Great Britain by Athenaeum Press Ltd, Newcastle upon Tyne.

Contents

List of Contributors

Mary Bogan is a business journalist with a specialist interest in women at work issues.

Anne Borrowdale is Social Responsibility Officer for the Oxford Diocesan Board and a writer of several books.

Bronwen Cohen is Director of the Scottish Child and Family Alliance and UK member of the European Commission Childcare Network.

Kathy Galloway works for the Iona Community and for Scottish Churches Action for World Development and is a writer and contextual theologian.

Margaret Halsey works as an industrial chaplain with South Yorkshire Industrial Mission.

Lesley Hart is head of the Senior Studies Institute of the University of Strathclyde in Glasgow.

Susan Hart is a member of the Woman's Group of Edinburgh District Council.

Hugh C Ormiston is Forth Valley Area Organiser with Scottish Churches Industrial Mission.

Sue Purves is a Personnel Consultant with ICI Pharmaceuticals.

Donald M Ross is the Industrial Mission Organiser of the Church of Scotland Board of National Mission.

Mary Ross is an educational psychologist and Director of the Notre Dame Centre for children, young people and their families in Glasgow.

Christa Springe is a pastor in Mainz with special responsibility for women and work issues in the Forum of European Women.

Yvonne Strachan is the Scottish Women's Organiser of the TGWU and a member of the STUC Women's Committee.

Elizabeth Templeton is editor of TRUST, the newsletter of SCM Press Trust, and co-ordinator of Threshold Theological Resource Project in Edinburgh.

Preface

LAVINIA BYRNE
and ERMAL KIRBY

Given our concern for the Community of Women and Men in the Church, and for Public Affairs, it is hardly surprising that we should be keenly interested in a publication that addresses the issue of women and work. In all the writing that deals with the world of work, there is very little about women, and even less *by* women: the Church of Scotland is to be commended for helping to remedy this deficiency.

This book is especially welcome because it deals, not only with justice, but with community. It makes clear that women have as much right to act in and influence the world, as men do, and that they must be treated equally in relationships—this is a matter of justice, but it also shows convincingly that the whole community benefits from 'feminisation', for the will to dominance and aggression is sinful and damages community.

One of the challenges faced by Christians in this field is to draw attention to pain and injustice without leaving readers and hearers so burdened by guilt that they cannot perceive the 'Gospel possibilities' of the situation. 'Inform the intellect, stir the emotion, move the will'—is a well-used formula for preachers and teachers, and the principles are applied here to good effect. The message is communicated by reasoned argument based on surveys, and by more evocative and personal writings that stimulate the imagination and emotion.

The practical difficulties experienced by women as they hold together the roles of carer and worker, are presented against the background of the flawed unequal relationship of women and men that has spanned so many centuries.

What this book offers is encouragement. It moves from the theoretical and analytical to the practical, and takes account of the glimmers of hope that are to be found therein. It has also helped us to consider more carefully what is 'A Woman's Place'. And so we warmly to all who seek justice and the strengthening of community.

Sr Lavinia Byrne IBVM
Associate Secretary
Community of Women and Men in the Church

Rev Ermal Kirby
Co-ordinating Secretary
Public Affairs

Council of Churches for Britain and Ireland
November 1992

Prologue

DONALD M ROSS
and HUGH C ORMISTON

[Feminist sensibilities about such a book having a male-written prologue should note that this is a companion volume to their earlier production, *New Patterns of Work*: 1990, Scottish Churches' Industrial Mission— *Editor.*]

In 1990 there were signs that the number of school leavers throughout the forthcoming decade would drop in number, leaving employers to face a labour supply shortage. One of our present contributors, Mary Bogan, for example, wrote, 'In October 1989 the Board of the TSB Group spotted a flaw in its five year business plan. How could it expect to hire and keep quality staff, when school leavers were in such short supply?'[1] Throughout the country companies were facing the same issue. At the same time, it was being said that this was the decade for women at work. There was much talk of 'women returners'. There was renewed discussion about companies providing creche facilities in order to encourage women back into the labour force.

All of this was accompanied by a resurgence of the debate about equal opportunities for women and men in the workplace. Conferences abounded, including one organised by Industrial Mission in Falkirk early in 1992. The Government launched its 'Opportunity 2000', of which there is some discussion in this book. At the same time a number of women took a decidedly jaundiced view of what was happening. Renewed interest in equal opportunities for women in the workplace was arising, in their view, not out of genuine concern for justice for women, but out of employers' fear of a shortage of young people in the labour market. Some women went so far as to say when the decade was over and the labour force more stable, then women would be discarded and their rights eroded.

Alas, what we have witnessed so far in the 90s has been Britain, along with the industrial nations of the world, plunging into the longest recession this century, a recession which at the time of writing this prologue threatens to become, in the view of some people, a full-blown slump. Now, as 1992 draws to a close, there is no talk of a labour force shortage, but instead, growing concern about escalating figures of unemployment, currently running at 9.6% for the nation as a whole.

Despite this unanticipated and certainly very different scenario from that envisaged at the beginning of the decade, the discussion of equal opportunities for women in the workplace continues. The Government's 'Opportunity 2000' scheme is still running and journals and newspapers can still be found publishing articles on the position of women in the workplace, It can therefore be argued that if public awareness of the position of women in the workplace can be heightened while unemployment is high and the country is in the throes of a very serious recession, the increase of opportunities for women at work are likely to be more permanent than if they had simply been the function of a very tight labour market. More importantly, if the rights of women at work can be improved and if women can be dealt with more justly and fairly in the workplace in terms of pay, conditions and career prospects at such a difficult time as the present, then these gains are likely to be more permanent than if they had emerged as a result of a very tight labour market.

In this book, Industrial Mission seeks to add to the debate by giving women a further opportunity to express their concern to an audience that my still need to be convinced of the justice of their case. That audience, we hope, will be one primarily comprising men. Women have made it clear that for them these issues have been of crucial importance for as long as they can remember. It is men who need to discuss them and it is men, primarily, who need to be convinced of the need for a change of attitude toward the employment of women in business and industry.

In Industrial Mission we have reflected, and continue to reflect the kind of bias towards male employment that has for a long time been a feature of many of the industries in which we have operated as industrial chaplains. Only for comparatively brief spells, it must be confessed, have women shared in the work of full-time chaplains, although there have always been a number sharing on a local or part-time basis. At one time this could be defended to some extent on the basis that the clergy of the Church was almost entirely male, but with some 25% of Church of Scotland ministers female and a similar figure in some of the other Reformed Churches, this argument can no longer be used.

Similarly, it could have been argued that Industrial Mission, 20 or 30 years ago, was strongest in the old, male-dominated, smoke-stack industries of Britain. But with their demise, this argument also can no longer be sustained, We too then, like the men with whom we meet on a daily basis in industry, need to listen again to the discussion put forward in this book, and to the arguments presented by our contributors, so that we, with men in industry, are moved to influence and change attitudes at work in favour of justice for women.

Life, however, is seldom if ever based on altruism. While there are good altruistic arguments for making sure that women have the same opportunity to earn a living and carve out a career as men, there are at least two hard-nosed powerful economic arguments for creating equal opportunities for women and men at work. The first of these takes account of the changing scene in management styles. Indeed, the whole world of work appears to be moving in a direction in which team working is central at every level, both on the shop floor and within management, and also across old skills and professional boundaries. The reason for this, of course, is the increased competitive forces which companies find themselves facing in the global market place.

Against this background there are very good arguments for suggesting that, in the Anglo-Saxon world at any rate, women have, by reason of upbringing, personality and social conditioning, greater gifts to bring to team working than men. Our Anglo-Saxon culture has traditionally emphasised individual attainment and individual leadership The new world of work seems to be suggesting that teams can achieve more than even high-flying, greatly gifted, individuals, and that women are better team workers, on the whole, than men.

Not only so, but many of the new teams in the world of work need a different type of management at the helm. There is less and less scope for the old autocratic style of management, and more and more scope for the kind of supportive, encouraging, mutually motivating style of management which, it is argued, women are uniquely gifted to develop. Jane McLoughlin, a former business editor of *The Guardian* and author of *Up and Running: Women in Business*, published by Virago, says:

Since the mid 80s, British business has had to face up to the fact that its management skills have been tried and found wanting. Traditional them and us techniques, typical of old style manufacturing industry, cut very little ice in the new technology and service areas—as many redundant executives discovered. The new emphasis was on co-operation and communication, rather than giving people orders and organising their man hours. Over the last five years emergency treatment—with Japanese ideas like 'team briefing'—was administered without any great success. Clearly, stronger medicine was required. So now, and with increasing enthusiasm, the brightest and best corporate thinking has embraced a process described (usually with an embarrassed laugh) as 'the feminisation of the business culture'.

McLoughlin summaries her view by saying, 'In my experience, women are much more co-operative than men. A lot of management training and theory now is, in fact, the feminine way of doing things,. Traditional practice was strong, authoritative, combative; now what a lot of training does is advocate communication and leading by example'.[2]

The second economic argument for increasing the number of women in the labour force and, indeed, for giving them equal opportunities with men is the straightforward observation that at a time of heightened competition, in particular, it is plainly stupid to ignore half the brain power and the potential in the population by making it overly difficult for women to compete for jobs with men. There are signs that while most people in private companies, and of course people who have been made unemployed, are only too well aware of the strength of competition facing people in the market place, many others in the public sector and others who choose not to be in the labour market, are not so aware of the strength of competitive forces in the contemporary world. While Karl Marx is now somewhat out of favour, he did correctly forecast that competition could only move in one direction—the direction of increasing ferocity. In his rather lurid military metaphor he wrote, 'The numerical increase of the capitals increases the competition between the capitalists. The increasing extent of the capitals provides the means for bringing more powerful labour armies with more gigantic instruments of war into the battle-field'.[3]

While we wish not to describe women as 'more gigantic instruments of war', in the competitive battle facing companies, no company that is determined to succeed and survive can possible ignore the increasingly large pool of highly educated women in the Western world and the increasingly large pool of women in Western society freed from the traditional burdens of the home to take their place in paid employment. Nor can they ignore the fact that Western societies have created the conditions whereby the majority of households are not content to exist on one wage, and the woman making themselves available for the labour market have as much if not more sense of commitment to paid employment than men.

Industrial Mission's approach to the subject of women and work is derived from an understanding both of our theology and the nature of work, neither of which is static. To those outside the Church, and perhaps for far too many within the Church, theology seems to be an unmoving body of inflexible doctrine. For Industrial Mission, and for many others in the Church, the excitement of theology is that it is not dead.

Our understanding of God is a developing understanding. There is now a healthy recognition in at least some parts of the Church that our understanding of human relationships with each other and with God, has been drastically curtailed and impaired by male imagery. It has seemed natural and appropriate to use terms like 'Lord' in addressing God, or 'Father', 'Master', 'King' or 'Brother', but this usage has been so dominant and so exclusive that our understanding of God's being, purpose, and will has been distorted.

The Church has been so shaped by this that its power structures, customs, and attitudes have been totally imbued with a male dominated authority. Only now is it being belatedly felt how much has been lost through this misunderstanding. It is a big 'if'—but if the Church had not so misunderstood the nature and character of God and so shaped its own life through male images and authority, its influence on politics, education, law, business, family and sexual relations would have been different. Had we realised more clearly that;

In the beginning God made the world
made it and mothered it
shaped it and fathered it
filled it with seeds and images of fertility
filled it with love and its folk with ability

the influence of the Church on society could have been different.

If we had heard Pope John Paul I more clearly when he said, just before his death, 'God is both Mother and Father, but more Mother than Father', then we would have been helped to a new view of creation and the environment, and a new view of human relationships in industry and society. There would have been a more female quality in the Church's influence on all aspects of society leading, arguably, to a more compassionate and caring order, better understanding of the creativity of individuals, and a wider understanding of human relations. This would surely have given rise to a vastly different world not least in the world of making, selling, building and trading. There would have been a greater emphasis on community, informality, nature and service. We would have lost our 'androcentric fallacy' and recognised that humanity consists of both men and women, and we would have discovered an equal, complimentary and matching partnership in work as well as in marriage.

The more we reflect on work itself and its importance for human beings as individuals in society and for the economy in general, the more we are aware of the changing nature of work. Indeed our recent book *New Patterns of Work* (available from Saint Andrew Press) was an exploration of this very subject. Most of the companies within which we worked consisted of a board made up entirely of men, male senior management, layers of male managers and foremen directing a virtually all-male workforce. In very few situations, but increasingly over the years, we began to encounter women. Here was the first dawning of insight for us. As we met women at work, again and again we discovered that the type of conversation we had with them was different from those which we were used to having with men. These differences were derived no doubt from the differences in psyche and experience between men and women and some of them are explored more deeply in later chapters of this book.

What is now clear to us is that women have a more realistic view of life. That is, they see their paid work as part of their total work. They do not divide life as radically as men into tidy sections. Their responsibilities as employees and their responsibilities at home are all part of that whole. Women can also see that while being an employee can be demanding, boring, or challenging, one of the key factors that makes work important for her is the ability to relate both to other women and to men within the place of employment. For women, the neighbour at home has a counterpart in the neighbour at work, and those relationships enrich the wholeness of her worklife.

In an earlier Industrial Mission publication, we compared the differences in the 'time clock' of a man's working experience with that of a woman. A man's progress through working life is strongly marked by the series of work-life situations which shape him; his early training years at college or during his apprenticeship; the gaining of qualifications; the use of his skill; the respect, responsibility or promotion achieved; seeing his old foreman retire; the trauma of redundancy; the period of unemployment; new starts in work and so on, possibly to the point of retirement and the unknown beyond. For a woman, the 'time clock' has far more relationship to domestic life intertwined with working life; the early years of work and training, marriage, the birth of her children, the return to work after children, relationships with older people, and the arranging of suitable work to fit in with domestic responsibility.

All of this may have been an exaggeration. Men too have a life beyond work and, increasingly, domestic responsibilities willingly assumed or otherwise. Perhaps, too, Victoria Klein exaggerates the role of women when she says, 'The lives of women are dominated by their roles as ever, by their roles as wives and mothers. Home and family are the focal points of their interest and are regarded by themselves, as well as by others, as their main responsibility. All other occupations are supportive to this central function'.[4]

Norman McKenzie, in his Australian study of this issue, is probably more accurate when he says, 'From childhood on, a girl is subject to a conflict of values. Marriage may be a goal, but it is no longer an exclusive goal. Before marriage, and increasingly sometime after marriage, she expects to play an independent economic role'.[5] At any rate it is probably the case that the woman's 'time clock' is a more appropriate time-keeper of life than that of the man's which has been so dominated by work-life demands.

The new patterns of working life which are evolving, and which are already here, involve a great deal of flexibility in the use of time, in the nature of work, and of contracts, and in the way people are paid. The new skills required, will call for a flexibility, which in the old male dominated world, simply did not exist. In this new phase of working life the experience of women will be valuable for the whole of working society, for working relations within employment, and for domestic life in the home. Both will be enriched by the reduction of the sharp division between work and home and between work and leisure.

Our concern in Industrial Mission is to seek a Christian perspective, and a Christian motivation and direction for the methods and goals of our industrial society. We are aware that industrial relations and industrial processes have been adversely affected by male dominance. Leadership has often been authoritarian, lacking in initiative and unwilling to admit to making mistakes.

Our hope is that this book will contribute to the development of new attitudes amongst men in the world of work, and that it will help to puncture false views of sexism. We justify Industrial Mission's sponsorship of the book on the grounds of justice and concern for the neighbour. It is clear that the age old question 'Who is my neighbour?' includes also the woman who stands alongside me. Whether that woman is for the man mother, wife, partner, girlfriend or simply acquaintance, he has a much moral duty to see that she is treated at least as fairly as he is, as he has of extending the concern to any other human being. As part of the work of the Church in Scotland, we do not need, therefore, to justify our support and encouragement for this publication or, indeed, for the subject to which it contributes. It is a question of extending justice to approximately half the population. Such is the enormity of that issue, it could rightly be argued that if justice is not extended to half the population, how can one expect justice to be extend to the many smaller groups based on race, religion or physical or mental condition. Indeed, we would argue that society's attitude to women is a measure of its morality, of how civilised it is, and of how serious in facing up to the demands of a more just future.

Finally a word of utmost appreciation to Elizabeth Templeton who has edited this volume, contributed to it herself, and chivvied, persuaded and otherwise cajoled all our contributors to deliver to a time, producing for Industrial Mission this contribution to the debate on the role and place of women in the world of work.

References

1   M Bogan: 'Let the Women Stand Up and be Counted', *Financial Times,* 25 November 1991.
2   J McLoughlin: "How does a Woman Manage?', *The Independent on Sunday,* 3 May 1992.
3   K Marx: 'Wage Labour and Capital', from Marx and Engels: *Selected Works in One Volume,* London, 1980, p 88.
4   *A Wee Worship Book,* Wild Goose Worship Group publication, 1989.
5   V Klein: *Britain's Married Women Workers,* Routledge & Kegan Paul, 1965.
6   E Sol and N McKenzie: *Women in Society—An Australian Study,* Malaby Press, 1975.

Part I
The Issues
Explored

1

Working out
our own Salvation

KATHY GALLOWAY

Of all the twentieth century revolutions, perhaps the most profound
and far-reaching will prove to have been that in the self-consciousness
of women. For the first time in history, the female sex, *as gender*, as
half the human race, has conceived of itself as subject and not object
of its own destiny. Women have become aware that they have the
right to define what it means to be a woman, and the right to refuse
imposed notions of identity. And all over the world, they are claiming that right.

Of course, this is not a uniform revolution, and by its very nature,
it resists all efforts to make it so. How women choose to identify
themselves, and where they choose to set priorities and invest ener-
gies varies enormously, is shaped and influenced by culture, class,
religion, geography, history and economics. Nor is it possible to draw
easy conclusions or make value judgements that do not risk being
facile, or enculturated within western notions of 'progress' and
'development'. The sight of thousands of Iranian women shrouded
from head to toe in black may be anathema to western women; to
the chador-wearer, it is a symbol of self-chosen identification. 'A
woman's right to choose' does not mean that women will make the
same choices, nor that they will necessarily be wise or approvable in
the eyes of others. Women, as men, are different from each other,
and will remain so. The point is, the right to choose for oneself, and
not simply be the object of other people's choices.

Nor is it by any means a completed revolution. One-third of the
world's women are still the *legal possession* of their male relatives.
But the revolutionary knowledge has entered into consciousness,
and, as in the Garden of Eden, it cannot be unlearned. In every country
in the world, there are women consciously and collectively choosing
to live as subject and not object of their own lives. And the great price
many of them pay for so doing simply demonstrates the revolutionary
knowledge to an ever-wider number.

3

But most importantly, it is not primarily a revolution in theory, but a revolution in practice. There are millions of women who would not use, or might even reject a feminist analysis or language who nevertheless act out of a new paradigm of what it means to be a woman. The clearest manifestation of this revolution in practice in Britain is seen in changing marital trends. One in three marriages in this country now end in divorce. Seventy-five per cent of these divorce actions are raised by women. Whatever the reasons for, and the implications of marital breakdown, it is clear that women in very large numbers are availing themselves of the opportunity to write the scripts for their own lives.

It is important, however, to differentiate freedom to choose and freedom to choose anything. The former is about the right to make our own decisions. The latter is about the options available to us in our decision-making. Claiming the former does not mean that the latter will be any wider or more palatable. Everyone operates within a continuum both of relative freedom to choose and of relative freedom of options to choose from, which affects men as much as women.

The women's movement has sought recognition of the right to be the subject, not the object of their own lives, as other liberation movements have sought that right for the poor and dispossessed, for black people, for homosexuals, for those defined from outside because of their nationality, political or religious beliefs. For many women worldwide, life has been, and remains a liberation struggle on many interrelated fronts, objectified as they are on the basis of gender *and* race *and* class. Simultaneously, and inseparable from this basic human right, has been the struggle to extend the range of meaningful choice. To use a rather crude metaphor, it has not simply been a question of women getting to the starting line, but also of seeking to remove the handicaps which so often leave them trailing.

It would be quite wrong to see that starting-line as being in a race for success, status, money or power, though sometimes it may feel that way to those who feel their own freedom (by which is often meant privilege) threatened by the refusal of others to buttress that freedom by fitting in with a particular world-view claimed as definitive. It is starkly clear that women are still a very long way from achieving anything remotely like parity, equality of opportunity or equality to take advantage of opportunity. Many of us are familiar with the oft-quoted United Nations statistics. Half the world's population is female. Two thirds of the world's work is done by women. They own one-tenth of the world's wealth, and one-hundredth of the world's land. Eighty per cent of the sweated labour employed by multi-national corporations in the Third World is female. The numerous wars and low-intensity conflicts throughout the world place a huge added burden on women, both as casualties and as primary carers. Land degradation, cash-cropping and industrialisation make it more and more difficult for women to pursue their traditional role as food-growers. The growing and interrelated problems of international debt and absolute poverty hit women and children first and hardest. The freeing of markets in Eastern Europe and the resultant soaring unemployment push women to the back of the line once again.

Even in Britain, where legislation (in the form of the Equal Pay Act and the Sex Discrimination Act) is already in existence which should in theory offer women greater equality of opportunity, practice and theory rarely coincide. Since these Acts were introduced in the 1970s, the gap in earnings between men and women has *increased*. World-wide, and in Britain, a combination of factors—recession; the concentration of women in low-paid, mainly female industries; lack of unionisation among women; and their role as primary carers which, among other things, pushes women into badly-paid and unprotected part-time work, has led to what is now recognised and known as the 'feminisation of poverty'.

No, the race is not for success. The race is overwhelmingly one for survival, for women and their children. And here is the first point where the gender factor is crucially important. For, though many of these other factors affect men just as much as women, though men are also powerfully oppressed by war, poverty, land clearance and discrimination, though relatively few men are in the race for success either, it is women's role as primary carers which, along with, and inextricably linked to cultural attitudes, defines their range of meaningful choice.

In Britain, although almost half the work force is female, domestic work and childcare is still overwhelmingly done by women. Women are also the large majority of those caring for elderly or disabled relatives. And as women increasingly exercise their choice to remove themselves from abusive or repressive marriages, that freedom has a high cost. In addition to the almost inevitable economic disadvantages, large numbers of women find themselves carrying the financial, emotional and physical burdens of parenthood alone. Ninety per cent of one-parent families in Britain have the mother as the one parent, and the majority of fathers cease fairly

rapidly to be in responsible contact, either personally or financially
with their children.

For tens of thousands of women in this country, 'working' means
entering a job market of low-paid and mostly (and increasingly) part-
time, unprotected employment, with no benefits, no security and
few prospects. For women with professional or high educational
qualifications it means having to prove themselves 'better than the
men', in order to be treated with parity—and even then there are few
guarantees, and the 'glass ceiling' that so often exists to stop women
being promoted above certain levels. For unqualified women, it means
concentration in low-paid mainly 'female' industries and services,
with little chance of training or promotion. And for most of them, it
means setting off to 'work' with at least 20 hours behind them of
that labour which is *still* so often not recognised as 'work'—the
cleaning, washing, cooking, shopping and caring which all but a
relatively small minority of women still carry the burden of. The
differentiation of women into 'working' and 'non-working' is unhelp-
ful and offensive, and bears no relation to the reality that all but the
most privileged women have worked and continue to work.

And for all women with children seeking paid employment, the
single biggest issue is the unending search for appropriate, affordable, reliable child care. The glossy magazine image of the power-
dressing woman executive, briefcase in hand, heading for the
boardroom, leaving her children safe in the hands of a trained nanny
is so far from the truth of most women's lives as to be laughably
irrelevant. The average woman in this country is much more likely to
be juggling relatives, friends, underpaid and under-resourced childminders and the faint hope of one of the few precious nursery places.

The irony in all this is that none of the difficulty faced by women
is actually based on trustworthy information. Research has tended
to show that women, including those with children, are actually more
reliable, less likely to take time off, than their male counterparts.
New studies support the view that female management styles, where
they are not forced into corporate mode, are often more effective and
more enabling for colleagues and employees. There are few (and
getting fewer) occupations where women are physically limited from
work that is as good as that of men.

There is, in fact, nothing to show that women, when they actually
get the chance, and are able to take advantage of it, perform less well
than men on a gender basis, In work terms, women are individuals in
the same way as men, and differences are likely to be on that basis

rather than on account of gender—except where cultural attitudes or practical obstacles tie their feet at the line.

Women have resolutely refused to see their children as obstacles (though others often see it this way). The majority of women will never put their work before their family commitments, though that does not mean that they are not ambitious, reliable or responsible. In fact, one might feel that the ability to assume responsibility for those unable to do it for themselves, and to refuse to sacrifice human nurture and wellbeing is a strength rather than a weakness, which should be valued for the personal qualities and maturity it develops, should be enabled as much as possible, and could do with being more widely shared.

No, the obstacles are the lack of appropriate, affordable and available child care (in which Britain lags behind every other EC country); the lack of training opportunities for women; the outright (although often subtle) discrimination against and harassment of women; and the inflexibility of so much working practice, which restricts women into low-paid jobs, often far below their ability, and renders part-time work risky, unequal and unprotected. Though many strides have been made, and women have leapt huge hurdles, they are running uphill all they way still. The annual report of the Equal Opportunities Commission for 1992 notes that the number of women reporting sex discrimination at work rose by 40% last year, complaints about dismissal for pregnancy by 50%, those related to sexual harassment by 30%, and those about equal pay by 20%. Joanna Foster, the EOC's chairwoman said that sex discrimination remained a major problem for women, exacerbated by the recession. She also said:

> We must keep equality at the top of the agenda. If Britain is not going to miss out on the economic advantages of the single market we must recognise the importance of our female workforce and go for high skills and top quality work. At the moment, our heavy dependence on underpaid women, and in particular on part-timers, means the government faces a choice. Ignore the gender aspect and lose out economically in the long run, or have a strategy for women in employment and make enormous gains.

This agenda is crucial for women at all points in their working lives, and in all strata of society, but more than anywhere else for the millions of women whose work is not primarily inspired by reasons of personal fulfilment, professional advancement or the largely illusory desire for 'pin money'. Women work because they want to, but mostly they want to because they have to. The average two-parent family now requires two salaries for the average mortgage. And for the large minority of families now living beneath the poverty line, many of them headed by women, it is an agenda which makes sense for women, for their children, and ultimately for industry and for the country as a whole.

Christianity is a faith founded on a gospel which announces good news to the poor, liberty to captives, recovery of sight to the blind, freedom to the oppressed, beginning right now. It believes in the unique and precious individuality of persons made in the image of God, male *and* female, and that that individuality is supremely called out and expressed in relationship, in community. It claims a God-gifted right for each person, without qualification or exclusion, to be the subject, not the object, of his or her own life and calling. It preaches justice and forgiving love as the means of realising the peaceable kingdom. Its followers, the church, are unfortunately some-times somewhat myopic to the fact that that requires a political agenda to redress the inequities perpetrated against all who are excluded from meaningful choice in the present social, economic and religious structures. And that, scoring highly among the excluded, are women. It is no longer (never has been) appropriate to define women by relationship to men. It is not the gospel. It seems incredible to have to repeat that women are people in their own right, with their own right to work out their own salvation (whether that includes religious faith or not). But it is a right still denied to them in practice in many arenas of life, including employment. When the revolution in practice meets the denial in practice, confrontation is inevitable. The courage, humility and readiness to change and to negotiate common ground that is necessary if the conflict is to be creative could be modelled, encouraged, by the church; women and men could be helped to dialogue, explore new patterns, support one another through the necessary changes. But will it be? Will they be? Perhaps this book is a small step in that direction.

2

Difficulties facing
Working Women

MARY BOGAN

Tailor-suited, immaculately groomed, attache case in one hand a clutch of company reports in the other, this is how the working woman is portrayed in popular culture. Her face adorns magazine covers; she's the star of TV commercials and drama series. She probably runs her own successful PR consultancy, sits on the board of a major plc and is frequently seen on our screens winging her way, executive-class, to a business meeting in New York or powering through open countryside in her sleek, open-top sports car.

The message is that working women now have power and status and salaries to reflect them. The reality, however, is somewhat different. Women many have learned how to dress for power in the workplace but few have managed to achieve it.

Whatever the ad world says, the average working woman in the UK still earns less money, has a lower status job, enjoys fewer employment benefits and has less chance of promotion than the average working man—and that's a situation which has changed little in recent years.

Women are not a rare species in the workforce. Almost as many women are in paid employment as men. According to the Institute of Employment Research, there are 21.8 million employees in Britain, of whom 45% are women. In fact, Britain now has a higher proportion of women at work than any other EC country. However, it also has the widest gap between men's and women's earnings in the Community.

In 1990, women who worked full-time earned, on average, only 77% of men's hourly pay and under 70% of men's Commission. Part-time women workers do even worse. Women full-timers earn less than male full-timers but women part-timers earn less for every hour worked than either. When you consider that 43% of women work part-time against 8% of men, it's clear that poor pay remains a major problem for working women as a whole but especially part-timers.

Linked with poor pay is women's concentration in low-status jobs. Women are less likely to be professionals, employers and managers than men and more likely to be in junior non-manual and lower level manual work.

Even when women do enter the professions and higher status jobs in significant numbers, however, they are still likely to do worse than men. For example, one survey of the nursing profession found that although over 90% of qualified nurses are women, 46% of Chief Officers are men. In the Civil Service, too, women represent nearly half of all employees but they are heavily concentrated in the lowest clerical grades. Just 7% of top Civil Service posts are filled by women.

Professional women are often paid less than professional men as well even though they may hold an equally responsible job. A study, undertaken last year by the Association of University Teachers, found that women professors are paid on average 2000 pounds a year less than male colleagues. The pay difference could be partly attributed to women's greater representation in 'softer' humanities disciplines—a common feature of women's pay patterns at work is that lower pay applies in areas in which women predominate—but the study also showed that women are comparatively poorly paid no matter which subject they teach.

So why is it women tend to be more disadvantaged at work than men regardless of the job they do and the level of career success they have achieved?

Broadly, there are two reasons. First, women find the climb out of junior and low-level positions tougher than men. Many get locked into dead-end jobs and are hampered in their progress by their employers' selection and promotion procedures which may well be based on outdated attitudes to women at work.

Second, the world of work has been designed by men for men. More specifically, it has been designed for a man married to a full-time wife and mother who can shoulder the burden of family life while her partner is free to work the long hours and dedication that many jobs demand in this competitive age.

These problems are not just the concern of high-flying women. Not every woman wants to run ICI, true, but given half a chance a significant number might prefer to be shop manager rather than shop assistant, section supervisor rather than production line worker. In all cases though, candidates have to successfully negotiate their way through employers' recruitment and promotion procedures—rarely the scientific, unbiased arbiters of ability they are supposed to be.

Getting promoted is typically harder for women than for men. Sometimes this is because women choose careers, like secretarial work, where progression prospects are few. (Whether this would change if more men became secretaries, however, is a debatable point. It is interesting that where men have chosen career paths that historically have not led to promotion opportunities, they have somehow managed to redraw the map and edge up the promotion ladder anyway.)

A good place to examine women's and men's promotion opportunities is on graduate management training schemes. These provide one of the few examples where men and women join an employer on a completely equal footing. Both sexes have similar academic achievements and have been selected according to common criteria.

In theory then, women's careers should progress as well as men's but in the few organisations in which promotion rates are tracked, the finding is that although men and women start their careers equally well, men pull ahead of women while they're still in their mid or late twenties. Most employers would argue that women only fall behind men once they have children but the evidence suggest that the disparity of opportunity between the sexes begins far too early in most cases to blame childbirth.

A more likely explanation is that bias is built into employer's recruitment and promotion procedures, albeit often unwittingly. One company, for example, found that women's lower promotion rates were partly explained by the fact that women were consistently rated as having lower potential for development than their male peers by their mainly male management team. Further investigations revealed it was managers' attitudes to women rather than women's lack of ability that was keeping them out of the promotion race.

Outdated attitudes clearly have a major impact on women's progress at work. Many employers still divide work into 'women's jobs' and 'men's jobs' and, as we've seen, jobs in which women predominate are almost, without exception, lower paid and lower status than comparable men's jobs.

It is for this reason that the Equal Opportunities Commission has been keen to institutionalise the principle of equal pay for work of equal value into the workplace. It forces employers to look analytically and objectively at the responsibilities and duties of each post and set pay accordingly rather than automatically assuming that women's work only merits women's pay.

Getting out out of low-paid, low-status work may be one problem facing working women but, more important still, there is the difficulty women have combining work with their family responsibilities. The workplace simply has not been designed to cater for employees who want gainful employment but also have caring duties in the home to perform. Increasingly, of course, this is not just a problem that affects women. There are now more women who are the main, or even sole, breadwinners in the family and more are returning to full-time work immediately after having their children. Men too are therefore finding it more difficult to combine work and home life.

Although society is changing, it is still women however who shoulder the lion's share of caring responsibilities in the home. The difficulties they face and the help they need though differs widely from one woman to another.

For mothers-to-be the concern may be poor maternity rights or ineligibility for maternity rights—in the UK women have to work for an employer for two years before they qualify for benefits. Pregnant women may also be concerned about keeping their jobs. The UK is the only country in the EC which does not give women the statutory right to return to work after having a baby.

For single parents and for those in low-paid employment, good quality, affordable child care may be the issue. Without it single parents are often forced to stay at home on social security to care for their children while inadequate child care provisions forces other mothers into low-paid, part-time jobs which hold little hope of advancement.

For a well-paid professional or managerial woman, however, the work/home conflict is different again. She is likely to less concerned about affording child care and more troubled by the task of reconciling the long hours and frequent travel her job demands with the desire to see her children.

The problem changes again when you consider who the woman is caring for. Women with babies and pre-school children clearly have different needs from those with school-age children while women who care for elderly relatives have different needs from mothers.

Given the high-profile success a handful of women have enjoyed in politics and industry, and the media world's eagerness to present a new powerful image of the working woman, it would be easy to think that the workplace is now a level playing field on which men and women compete freely and equally. Unfortunately, that is still not the case. Working life for the majority women has changed little in recent years. Poor pay, poor promotion prospects and poor child care provision continue to dog working women as much now as they did at the beginning of the shoulder-padded, power-dressed eighties. The picture is *not* completely bleak however. Not only has the government declared itself committed to bringing down the hurdles facing working women but, more importantly, a growing number of employers are acknowledging that women do not get a fair crack of the whip at work. Slowly but surely companies are beginning to appreciate the valuable talent they have wasted and take steps to redress the balance. If there was ever a time for removing inequality in the workforce once and for all—this is it.

3

Women at Work

Patterns of Race and Gender

MARGARET HALSEY

Women's Work in the Labour Market—A Brief Overview

For much of the nineteenth century a working woman was almost by definition working class; in today's popular mythology a working woman in a 'superwomen' ensconced in a professional career. Neither could be further from the contemporary reality.[1]

Since the industrial revolution, women have always been part of the paid labour market—in 1850 they formed 31% of the working population, and the proportions remained approximately the same until 1950. The last 40 years have seen considerable changes in the labour market; and thus their participation has changed considerably; in 1961 working women formed 36% of the total and in 1981 40.2%. If the latest predictions about demographic changes are accurate, it is likely that women are likely to be encouraged to form an even greater percentage of the working population during the last decade of the twentieth century.[2]

However a more thorough analysis of the statistics—which indicate where women are to be fond in paid employment—suggest that equality of opportunity is still be be realised. From this perspective, women's participation in paid employment presents a somewhat depressing picture in two major ways.

First, the increase in the numbers of employed women does not reflect an increase in the variety of work which they do. The majority of women are employed in a narrow range of industrial occupations —in the service industries, mainly in clerical catering and cleaning work; in manufacturing industries predominantly in food drink and tobacco, footwear and textiles, and light engineering.[3]

Within the professions too, there is considerable occupational segregation. Eighty per cent of primary school teachers are women, and 44% of secondary. One per cent of civil engineers, judges and university professors are female, 2% of accountants, 3% of MPs, 6% of solicitors and 13% of managers.

Second, women who reach the most senior positions in industrial or professional life tend to be the exception rather than the rule. Although women make up 80% of primary school teachers, 56% of primary heads are male and 44% female; in the nursing profession, a third of the most senior nursing posts are held by men, who make up but 10% of the total nursing population. In the trades and industries where women employees outnumber men, women hold under 10% of the most senior posts.[4]

Inevitably there are exceptions to these generalisations, and some women do 'succeed' in terms of their employment prospects to occupy key positions. But in describing professional occupations, many have argued that:

> The acceptance gained by professional women in the past, has been the acceptance of an exceptional individual, rather than the acceptance of women as a professional group..Often this has been gained by women making some harsh personal choices—such as sacrificing marriage or a family.[5]

If such personal choices are the prerogative of the professional women however, how much harder is it for women whose choices are more limited?

Work and Home—A Brief Historical Overview

> The paid jobs that women do outside the home, tend to be very similar to the unpaid jobs they do inside the home—such as cleaning, sewing, washing and cooking.[6]

The ways in which employment is divided within the paid labour market are also mirrored in the divisions and types of jobs which women do in the domestic sphere of life—unpaid and at home. Several writers have argued that the devaluation of domestic work was one of the major features of mass industrialisation, though Rosemary Ruether has suggested that for women there was an earlier critical turning point in their socio-economic history—that of the transition from village to urban life.[7]

It could well be argued that in Western civilisation there has always been a division of labour which is related to gender—since men had tended to be occupied in hunting and women in gathering tasks to supply food for the family. However women still played a part in the economic life of a community, by virtue of the fact that they were involved in initial forms of agriculture, production of herbal medicines, baskets and pottery.

The transition to an urban form of life however meant a transition to a way of life in which some men gained a greater sense of political power through their participation in the 'public' decision making sphere. Ruether argues that the combination of this political power, and the ways in which gender divided labour combined to devalue women's 'status' in the world of work.

A more widely accepted theory however, places industrialisation as more centrally important in the ways in which domestic work became devalued. The advent of mass employment in factories, separated the home from the workplace—the latter becoming the place of production, and the former the place of consumption. The consequence of this for married women, (or their equivalent) was that in domestic terms they became economically dependent on men for their survival.

This pattern of economic dependence was further reinforced by the ways in which women were involved in producing and rearing children—which in the period before effective contraception, tended to involve a greater proportion of a women's life than in contemporary society.[8]

The period after the industrial revolution, saw many poorer women, often of rural origin, working within garment and textile industries, and domestic service too provided a source of employment. As Tilley and Scott have indicated, for women of a 'lower socio-economic status' female paid labour was an economic necessity for the survival of their families. However, whilst the location of such labour changed, its essential gender divisions reflected traditional stereotypes.[9]

Tilley and Scott point out that the patterns of women's paid work across Europe during the late nineteenth century reflect a complex response to industrialisation, on the part of different socio-economic groups. The changes in women's work during this period were however rooted in the family values—and thus the divisions of labour in paid employment, reflected those which were essentially also true of the home.

Women at Work—Some General Issues;

Women's jobs are stratified into what can look like two different worlds; at the one extreme the growing army of part-time workers, disproportionately concentrated in 'women only jobs' in saleswork, cleaning and canteens ... at the other the women who have been through higher education, who have full-time and relatively powerful jobs earning wages that are good if not brilliant for a man. And somewhere in the middle, the fragile bridge of office workers.[10]

Anne Phillips' summary of the ways in which women are occupied in paid employment, illustrates one of the difficulties of exploring women's work—since it encompasses such a varied range of occupations. Clearly time and space preclude an exhaustive survey of the varieties of work which women may do—and thus considerable selection has been made in order to explore some of the issues which face women at work.

Recognising the risk of over-generalisation, this section has drawn out some characteristics of women's work which are features of industrial society in Britain. These relate predominantly to the ways in which work is organised, in terms of how people are paid, what hours they work, and whether their work is regarded as 'skilled' or 'unskilled' and women's attitudes to redundancy.

The recent expansion in the service sector of industry has created many jobs which are characteristically low paid, part-time and semi-skilled, which reflect many of the above. A detailed exploration of this area is outwith the scope of this essay, although it should be noted that many areas of women's employment have changed considerably as a result.

In selecting criteria for discussion, this essay has chosen to focus on the 'formal' industrial economy; and not explored the informal economy and the phenomenon of homeworking in detail. Further it concentrates on aspects of work where women are more 'vulnerable' in paid employment, whilst inevitably recognising that such characteristics do not apply to all women at work.

One of the features of women's employment is that for those who have children, the process of bringing them up may mean that they move in and out of paid employment, and thus may cross 'traditional' boundaries between jobs. In the 1980 Women and Employment survey, 45% of the women interviewed commented that the job which they occupied after their first child was of a 'lower status' than they had previously occupied; only 13% said it was higher. This has interesting consequences for the ways in which some women may understand class, and thus albeit disputably, Ann Phillips comments:

> Downward mobility is one of the facts of life for many women, and over the course of a lifetime, it can erode once powerful social barriers. Many women simply cannot afford the same sense of class as men, for the reality of their lives constantly contradicts it.[11]

Patterns of Paid Work:

> I think I'm worth at least £2.00 an hour. It's not enough to live on, but if I was going for a part-time job, I definitely wouldn't work for less.[12]

In 1988 the average full-time earnings of women were £164.20 per week, compared to £245.80 for men and thus on average, women's earnings were two thirds those of men. Research has suggested that women are heavily represented at the lower end of pay scales, almost invariably earning less than their male counterparts in 'equivalent' jobs.

According to the New Earnings Survey of 1985, 27% of female manual workers, and 10% of female non-manual workers earned a gross wage of less than £80 a week, compared with 2.4% and 1.6% of male manual and non-manual workers. This was well below the level of £110 per week, which made people eligible for family income supplement at the time.

Thus in general women are paid less then men for the work they do and also tend to be concentrated at the lower end of the pay scales. Within these generalisations there are a number of variations.

Since women who bear and bring up children, often do not work continuously throughout their life, they may opt out of the labour market and return to it at a lower level than men of equivalent age. This is in part an explanation for the fact that female earnings as a percentage of male, drop significantly between the ages of 18 and 49.[13]

Many women with domestic responsibilities also work fewer hours than men—the average hourly week for men in 1988 was 42.1 hours and for women 37.6. If these differences are taken into account, there is less discrepancy between the two sets of average earnings. The practice of paying overtime and bonus payments has in general tended to favour male employees rather than female.

One of the most significant factors in pay differentials is that of job segregation. Susan Lonsdale argues that the result of this is that a different wage structure has developed for women and men, keeping women's wages lower; and further indirectly removed women's jobs from the equal pay policy established in 1970. Further she argues that the result of these pay differentials, means that women and men make different judgements about their status and abilities in material terms—for example in 1985 a women in the top 10% of female earners would be earning £189.50 whereas a man would be earning £296.30.

This situation in Britain takes place in a context where an increasing proportion of families are dependent on two wages—the number of families classified as living in poverty would treble if it were not for the fact that both husband and wife were earning. Since one in eight households are headed by a single parent and 91% of these are women, it can no longer be assumed that families always consist of a breadwinning father and housewife mother. Finally in some 400,000 families in Britain, women are the main earners, because their partners are unemployed. In the words of one:

> I've always worked because I've had to I don't know where the idea that women work for pin money comes from.[14]

Part-time Work

> I found a shop job, as a checkout operator. It was part-time, five afternoons a week and I got about £34. Anything was better than nothing.[16]

One of the effects of changing patterns of industrial employment in the last ten or fifteen years in Britain, has been the growth of part-time work, In manufacturing industry this has enabled production to be kept continues, and often made the best use of capital equipment; in the service industry—particularly retailing and catering, this has enabled firms to respond to the irregularities of trade in peak periods. Thus for employers, part-time work increases the possibility of efficiency, productivity and profitability.

Full-time work has been defined as work which takes place for thirty hours a week (or 25 hours a week in the teaching profession); thus by deduction, part-time work can be regarded as work which takes place for less. On one level it apparently presents an attractive option for women combining paid work with family commitments—and Britain, the proportion of women who work part-time is 44% of the total female workforce.

Although one in five women who work part-time do not have specified basic hours of work, it has been estimated that the average numbers of hours they work per week is 19.4. However this conceals a wide variation—ranging on average from 10.4 hours in jobs such as school helpers, to 18.5 hours in jobs in the retail trade, and 23.2 hours for nursing auxiliaries

But although part-time work may present an apparently attractive proposition for women with domestic responsibilities, one of its consequences is a reduction in employment rights and protection offered to employees. Protection against unfair dismissal, entitlement to maternity benefits, and possibility of redundancy payment are only offered to those who have work for over 16 hours a week or for those working 8 hours a week for five years. Those who work for under 8 hours a week do not have such rights. Thus is has been estimated that about 38% of part-time workers have little or no employment protection.

Further, studies of trends in part-time employment suggest that the hourly earnings of women in part-time employment are declining in relative terms, when compared with those who work full-time. If in addition, employers keep wages below the level at which they become liable for National Insurance contributions, this may further restrict women's rights to claim social security benefits. Often too, part-time work excludes employees from pension schemes and sick pay.

Thus the intricacies and details of employment legislation have often worked against the interest of part-time workers, and are often to immediately apparent to those who take on part-time work. In general terms however, if links between employer and employee are more tenuous, employees have less legal protection and security. Often such a situation does not become apparent to part-time workers, until it may be too late.

I don't think we were enlightened enough to know what the benefits of the full stamp were. That is where they got away with it, isn't it?[16]

Understanding of Skill

The woman in a skilled job in the manufacturing or production industries is a rarity; around one quarter of female manual workers are in skilled occupations compared with over one half of males.

In a recent survey of the food industry which covered over 8000 people, GMB found that in 70% of the job grades, there were no women—which predominantly represented the more 'skilled' jobs in the workplace. this bears out the finding that in many industries, women are often to be found doing the more 'unskilled' jobs.

One factor which contributes to this, is the way in which training may operate, and another the way for married women, its accessibility may be affected by their domestic commitment. A third may undoubtedly be the job aspirations of women themselves. However some of this may also be explained by the understandings of 'skill' which have operated historically at work.

One way in which understanding so skill have been formed, is in association with the ways that production operates. For example, a recent study has compared the making of paper boxes by women on hand fed machines—paid and regarded as unskilled labour, with that of cartons on a more highly automated process done by men—which is paid and recognised as semi-skilled.

A second difficulty in assessing skill, arises from situations in which new kinds of labour may be created. Anne Philips and Barbara Taylor cite the example of office clerical work—which expanded after the First World War. Previously Work as clerks in offices had been carried out by men, but the ways in which clerical work developed meant that it became very different,. Women who entered clerical work during this period, could not compare their work with their male predecessors—and some have argued that their work became 'downgraded' in terms of its skill components.

A third aspect of skill definition, has also been associated with the environment in which similar work is carried out. A study of the English clothing industry by Ben Birnaum has illustrated the ways in which machining work done by women in a more sub-divided labour process, has been regarded as semi-skilled, whereas that done by men in smaller shops machining different garments has been accorded skill status.[18]

Links between gender and skill are complex, partly formed because of changes in production processes, and partly because some groups of workers have struggled to retain their own status at the expense of others.

Exploring the ways in which understandings of skill changed within an all-women's clothing factory, Sallie Westwood described how the need to produce clothes more quickly began to take precedence over the quality of production, and the ways it was organised. Yet for the women concerned, understandings of skill had much to say about their own dignity:

> This bonus system gives you the money if there is work and you are quick, but it doesn't allow for the skill in the work. You can be really good and it makes no difference, it's speed they want.[19]

Women and Unemployment

> Work is company, it's meeting people. When I've been working I've quite enjoyed it but when I'm out of work it's not very nice. When I'm working at least I know I've got some money of my own to spend.

Many studies of married women in employment, point to two important positive factors which lead them to seek work. One is the possibility of a greater sense of economic autonomy and the other the potential for relationships outside the isolation of the home. The numbers of married women who are in paid employment has thus increased steadily since the early 1950s.

Within the last twenty years there have been two contradictory trends in employment which have affected women in ambiguous ways—job losses in manufacturing industry, and the expansion of jobs in the service sector. Thus the effects of former have to some extent been masked by the expansion of the latter.

Although the rate of unemployment amongst women between 1974 and 1978 was officially calculated as rising more than three times that of men, this may well have been overestimated because of the way that figures were calculated. Nonetheless the ways in which some firms operate a redundancy policy, may have indirectly discriminated against women in several areas.

First the principle of 'last in first out' may discriminate against women whose experience of employment is discontinuous. Second women working in jobs requiring lower levels of 'skill' may be made redundant in contrast to more skilled male workers whom employers consider to be less easily replaced. Third women working on 'twilight shifts' in firms, may find that their labour can be dispensed with, in times of recession. These factors make women vulnerable to unemployment in different ways from men.

At the same time, underlying social assumptions about women's domestic responsibilities, may contribute to understandings that unemployment is more of a social and personal problem for men than it is for women. Thus often women's confidence in their 'right' to work is lower than that of men—and in some instances high unemployment amongst other vulnerable groups in society has been set against the increasing tendency of married women to seek paid employment.

Further, many women who are made redundant do not register as unemployed—which makes accurate levels of unemployment hard to evaluate. In her study of women made redundant from a clothing factory in West Yorkshire, Angela Coyle discovered that the ways in which women restricted their availability for work—often to tie in with domestic commitments, might disqualify them from taking up job offers, and thus from continuing to receive unemployment benefit. As one commented:

> I did register. I started getting unemployment benefit ... but I got suspended for refusing two jobs, so they didn't bother and I haven't bothered with them ... I still look in the job centre though.

Links between Race and Gender—Examples from Areas of Women's Employment

> I worked because my husband was unemployed. I thought if I do something at least it's an income.[22]

This section explores four areas of women's employment in order to consider the ways in which work is affected by their racial origin. Such links are complex—for they depend both on the industry in which women work, and the attitudes of the different ethnic communities from which they originate.

Three of the four areas of work make links between race and gender in Britain, where government policy on immigration also affects women's employment. The fourth area discusses the way that multi-national companies 'contract' work out to developing countries—where labour is cheaper than in Britain—thus illustrating links between work race and gender need to be considered in a global context.

Within Britain, amongst women who are 'economically active', a high proportion of women of West Indian or Asian origin have a full-time job—in 1981 calculated at 62.2% and 61% respectively, compared with the 41% of white women in full-time employment. Within different religious communities, there is also considerable variation—for example women of Muslim origin are less likely to be in full-time work outside the home than Sikh women.

The kinds of work which black women do also differs from those of British origin; Asian women for example are more likely to be working in the family businesses in the clothing or catering trade, and West Indian in engineering trades or the Health Service.[23]

For some women the possibility of homeworking—sewing or packing jobs contracted out by some major retailers, has provided one way in which they have found an income in working from home. The exact estimate of the numbers of women employed in this way is hard to evaluate, although their pay and working conditions are often worse than those working in other sectors of the economy.

The major reason given by black women for seeking work is often that of finance. In Britain, high unemployment rates among black men (the overall average unemployment rate of black men was calculated as 20% compared with 10% white in 1987), may mean that women may seek work—as illustrated by the examples given at the outset. However, since on average black men earn less than white, a second income may be invaluable to support the family.

Further, many women who work also have obligations to families beyond the immediate nuclear network. In a survey in which black women in West Yorkshire talk about their working lives, many commented on the wider responsibilities to families in Asia Africa or the Carribean:

I'm widowed—my husband died at 45 with meningitis, and I've to support my mother in the West Indies. She's 95. So me works and me works.[24]

(i) The National Health Service

> I like nursing. I'm used to it. But I will tell my children to do something else. I don't think nursing is respected in the community.[25]

The National Health Service is the largest single employer in Western Europe, and the largest employer of black people in this country. Current estimates suggest that the proportion of black nurses in the service stands at approximately 9%, and thus it is one area in which black women might be considered to be 'well represented' in a professional occupation.

When the NHS came into being, in 1948, a number of health workers were recruited from overseas to fill the staff vacancies which had been created. The health service was exempted from the Immigration Acts of 1962 and 1965, in order to maintain the recruitment of trainee and auxiliary nurses. However, the Immigration Act of 1971 ended the automatic right of entry to prospective nurses, and by 1983, work permits were withdrawn, and thus overseas nurses were no longer being recruited to work in the NHS.

Yet despite the fact that the health service employs a high percentage of black women, the majority are to be found either in the 'lower grades' of the nursing profession, or working as ancillary staff in cleaning and catering. in a study of the working conditions of black nurses in West Yorkshire's hospitals, Marie Lee-Cunin found a number of obstacles to their promotion prospects.

One obstacle was to be found in the provision of training. Currently within the nursing profession, there are two levels of training—SEN and SRN qualifications. Studies of the qualification levels of black nurses, have borne out the comment of one:

> Most West Indian nurses went onto the SEN course. It didn't matter how many qualifications you had, you went on the SEN course. They didn't encourage you to do the SRN.[26]

Further, many black nurses tend to be concentrated in the less popular areas of employment within the health service. Figures most recently obtainable from the General Nursing Council, indicate that nearly one third of black student nurses are to be found in psychiatric nursing, and many nurses interviewed in the survey suggested that white people did not chose to work in these 'dead end' areas of the profession:

My new ward was a psychiatric ward. It was bad ... a most trying place. The majority of people working on the ward were black. I feel that we maintained that stability.[27]

A third feature of much black women's employment in the health service was that of unsocial hours. Many nurses in the survey worked night shifts, partly because this would provide extra money, and in some circumstances the opportunity for promotion. However the main reason which most gave for this form of work was that it could be combined with care of children:

I did it for the children. When they went to sleep then I would go to work. The children are the important ones.[28]

(ii) The Fast Food Industry

Catering makes you very cut off from other people. The only time you have off is when most people are in bed, and when most other people are off, that's when you're working hardest ....[29]

The 'fast food' industry in Britain had its historical roots in the demand for industrial catering which was a feature of the second world war. Post-war economic expansion saw the growth of 'service' industries throughout this country, and during the 1970s and 80s there was considerable expansion of the 'fast food' chains—for example Macdonalds.

This development and change in the catering industry coincided with the changing patterns of immigration of Chinese people to Britain. Chinese immigration dates back to the eighteenth century, but with the establishment of the Maoist government in China, and the rapid industrialisation of Hong Kong, many more immigrants came to Britain as a result of the post war economic boom and need for labour in this country.

I came to England, because you couldn't get a job in Hong Kong to put food into our mouth. My uncle worked in a restaurant ... he signed the form for me to come.[30]

British immigration policies of the 1960s and early 70s had two major effects on Chinese (and other) immigrants. First they had to rely on sponsorship from Chinese people in Britain, and second that men were permitted to bring their wives and dependants with them, whereas women were not. Many women thus found work in the growing Chinese restaurant business.

> When I came here in 1968, I went to live with my husband, above my uncle's takeaway shop for a year. We both worked there in the evenings, and he gave us free food and didn't ask for any rent. Oh no we didn't get paid.[31]

For Chinese women, this presented a particular series of difficulties. Many were faced with inadequate housing, and worked in family business as kitchen workers or cleaners in exchange for accommodation. Later, when competition from fast food chains, forced restaurants to turned their work over to Chinese take-away businesses, the demands of work for some became incompatible with bringing up children. As one child commented:

> I was actually born here you know. But you wouldn't think so. I lived with my auntie in Hong Kong from when I was a baby until I was eight.[32]

Whereas for some women the possibility of becoming partners in their husband's business, had offered them a greater sense of economic autonomy than they might have had otherwise, many are only too aware of its precarious nature, its long and unsocial hours, which may bring relatively little reward. This had led many of them to wish for a better future for their children:

> I'll tell you one thing. I don't want this life for my daughter. I want better for her. I want her to speak English, and get a good job.[33]

(iii) The Clothing Industry

> I see the majority of women working for me as benefiting from my job offer. They are illiterate and they have no skills, hence no British factory will make use of them .... Their £20 a week will help toward the family income—and we are like one big family here.[34]

The vulnerability of immigrant women in the industrial changes of the first decade, is illustrated clearly by the above quotation by an Asian entrepreneur in Coventry. Many women have found work within their 'ethnic community' which in some instances provides a culturally 'safer environment'. Further language and 'skill' do not present the same obstacles to employment which they might experience elsewhere.

The increases in the numbers of such smaller scale enterprises, has been the result of the decline in the numbers of people employed in manufacturing industries in Britain during the 1980s. This had led many of those made unemployed to seek alternative forms of employment in small businesses. This option—encouraged by current government policy, has been taken up in particular by members of the Asian community, and was one way in which victims of the recession could 'secure a stake in their community'.[35]

The production of clothing is one example of the ways in which some immigrant groups have found a niche in the British economy. Recently the redundancy payments offered by manufacturing industries, have given some enough capital to set up a small business. Production can be carried out more cheaply by paying low wages, and evading employment legislation, and this ensures that goods can be cheaply produced, and quickly delivered to retailers meeting unpredictable demands of the fashion market.

In her investigation of this part of the clothing industry in the West Midlands, Annie Phizackles points out that the experience of racial discrimination and harassment which many Asian people have felt in Britain, may in itself encourage 'ethnic solidarity'; further the use of women's skills as a form of cheap or unpaid labour has been a vital factor in contributing to their development.

Further, the investigation illustrates that often such a form of production takes place within a cultural context of a clear understanding of the sexual division of labour. Women's employment is condoned if it does not threaten that of the male head of the family, nor jeopardise the care of children. in such a context, women and men have different expectations of their jobs, complementing their understandings of gender.

In some instances production has been carried out within a family firm, where women have been employed as machinists, finishers and supervisors; but in other instances, work can be carried out by homeworkers, whose employment situation can be even more precarious:

I am a widow, and I really do not know what my legal status is. If

I apply for cards and things, I may be asked to leave the country. At the moment my uncle brings machine work to my home. It works out at 50 pence an hour. But I earn, and I feed my children somehow. Most of all I do not have to deal with the fear of racist abuse in this white world.[36]

(iv) The International Labour Market

The manual dexterity of the oriental female is famous the world over. Her hands are small and she works fast with extreme care. Who therefore could be better qualified by nature and inheritance to contribute to the efficiency of a bench assembly line than the oriental girl.[37]

The above extract from a Malaysian investment brochure, was designed to attract foreign firms to relocate their production to an environment where its costs would be lower. This strategy is one which has been adopted by some American, Japanese, or European multinational companies, who may sub-contract to a 'Third World' factory, and take responsibility themselves for the marketing and sale of the product. It has become a characteristic of some of the production of garments, textiles and components for the electronics industry.

This system which has been in operations since the late 1960s, often relies heavily on a labour-intensive process. Since wages in the 'third world' can be up to ten times lower, there may be fewer employment restrictions, and thus a greater degree of potential control over those who work in such an environment. Thus firms who are able to relocate their work in this way, have the potential for greater profitability.

Studies of this practice have indicated that those who work in such factories are very often young women between the ages of 15 and 20. Often companies who work in this way may pay women less than men, and consider them to be a more 'adaptable' workforce. As important the fact that young women may have learned to sew at home, means that they require little training. Such skills can be used in industrial garment making, or may be quite similar to those needed to assemble electronic components.

However this group of woman may be vulnerable to unemployment—in two ways. A recession in a 'first world' country may lead to mass unemployment in the third world, with little sense of accountability to the workforce concerned; secondly the preference of local firms for younger workers, may mean that those who have not left voluntarily in their mid twenties may be dismissed. Health and safety conditions in the factories concerned, may lead to the deterioration of eyesight, and fatigue—which may lead to a deterioration in their performance at work.

This analysis needs to be understood not only in terms of employment conditions but also in terms of attitudes to gender—often rationalised as 'natural' by employers. Many have argued that women in such circumstances occupy a 'secondary status' in the labour market, their primary role being one which is domestic and linked to producing and rearing children. Young women can thus be asked to work in such conditions to supplement a family income, prior to fulfilling their traditional role as wives and mothers.

Studies of young women employed in a Singapore textile factory illustrated the ways that women who were characterised as 'naturally docile' employees, had learned to be subservient in the presence of supervisors, but in their absence their behaviour changed. Employers' claims that 'docility' is a 'natural' female trait thus need qualifying![38]

Diane Elson and Ruth Pearson have explored several of the ways in which third world manufacturing of this type reduces ambiguity and conflict for women employees. On the one hand such employment is precarious and temporary, yet on the other work outside the home may offer some young women the possibility of some economic autonomy and in some circumstances the possibility of 'escape' from an arranged marriage.

In some areas, large multinational companies have increased this sense of conflict—for example the large American multinational companies which provide 'fringe benefits for their employees' in the form of fashion and beauty care, and westernised social functions. However as Elsdon and Pearson point out, employees here may have exchanged 'one form of gender subordination to fathers and brothers for another form of subordination to their male bosses'. Almost without exception, patterns of employment in such companies, show that young women are employed at the lowest levels of work, and their managers and supervisors are predominantly male.

At the other end of the spectrum, some companies working in this environment aim to preserve traditional cultural values and to reinforce the traditional values of culture and gender. One such example is to be found in the attempts of one company to integrate its workplaces with traditional values—as advertised in its brochure:

> The company has installed prayer rooms in the factory itself, does
> not have modern uniforms, but lets the girls wear their traditional
> attire, and enforces a strict and rigid discipline in the workplace.[39]

The Inter-connectedness of Work:
Some Theological Reflections

> The saying 'a woman's work is never done,' reflects the extent of
> women's responsibilities. It is true that most work is 'never done'
> unless a decision is made to stop or one leaves the workplace ...
> For a woman with domestic responsibilities, it is (even more)
> difficult to escape the knowledge of work to be done. She must
> sit in the unbrushed armchair, watching the undusted television,
> creating washing up as she drinks her coffee, and constantly
> listening out for the children.[40]

Women's experience of work encompasses both the private and
public areas of life—and thus needs to be understood in this context.
Married women in particular may find themselves doing two jobs—
one which is paid outside the home, and another often 'voluntary'
within it. Any theological understanding of women's work must thus
straddle the divide between the 'domestic' and 'industrial arenas'.

Often the domestic work which women do is 'hidden' from public
view, and is characteristically anonymous (although this feature may
be shared with some men). This sense of hidden-ness also pervades
many of the paid jobs in which women are employed—the most
striking illustration being that of cleaners who sweep offices before
the arrival of those who work there, or those in catering whose work
involves long hours out of sight.

Understandings of women's work, thus need to take seriously
that in many cases it is unrecognised. This has thus led some women
to argue that theological understandings of work needs to take
seriously both its 'private and unpaid' dimension as well as its
'public and paid'. Exploring a new model for the theology of work,
Elizabeth Nash argues:

> A new theology of work needs to begin with a new definition of
> work. To count only the work we are paid for, is no longer

adequate. We need a way of understanding work in much wider terms. For myself I am unable to divide my life unto paid working life' and 'unpaid working life'. My responsibilities at home, and my responsibilities as an industrial chaplain are a confused lump of 'life'. I perceive life as a whole, because I am one person, and each part of my life relates to every other.[41]

This understanding of work—with its emphasis on wholeness', may be criticised in that the width of its definition may be too all encompassing. Whilst its advantage lies in its inclusiveness, it may well leave little room for distinguishing between 'work' and 'leisure'. Yet at the same time, Anne Borrowdale's realistic analysis of the domestic lives of many women, quoted above, illustrates the fact that many women's lives leave little room for the latter.

If wholeness and inter-connectedness, is applied to an understanding of individual women's working lives, then Elizabeth Nash argues that the valuing of work needs to be understood in terms of the qualities of relationship it reflects. Work is not to be understood as an end in itself, but rather in the context of human beings' interactions with each other. One way of theologising about women's work may be to explore some characteristics of this relatedness—and thus the remainder of this section explores four such characteristics.

Work and Value

The protest of the gospels at the concrete sociological realities in which maleness and femaleness are elements, along with class, ethnicity, religious office and law which define social status.[42]

The preceding sections have explored in some detail the ways in which for many women in paid employment their work is valued less highly than that of their male counterparts. understandings of 'skill' for example often illustrate ways in which 'domestically acquired skills' are given less 'industrial' value than those gained through industrial training programmes. In material terms, women's work is in general less highly paid than men's. And on the whole many women occupy jobs of a lower 'status' than those of their male counterparts.

This understanding of 'value' is further highlighted by the ways in which race and gender interact. The experiences of black women in Britain, and that of young women working in some sections of the labour market abroad, illustrates the ways in which economic relationships reinforce such disadvantages of race and gender.

Rosemary Ruether argues that the sociological realistics of gender and race are central to understanding of value. She argues that Jesus spoke and acted as a critic of religious and social hierarchies, aiming to establish a new social order. in this context women play an important 'representative part' in Jesus' criticism of status relationships, in which he argues that 'the first shall be last and the last shall be first':

> Women play an important role in this Gospel vindication of the lowly in God's new order. It is the women of oppressed and marginalised groups who are often pictured as the representatives of the lowly. The dialogue with at the well takes place with a Samaritan women. A Syrophoenecian woman is the prophetic seeker who forces Jesus to concede redemption of the Gentiles Among the poor, it is the widows who are most destitute.[43]

Ruether's understanding of 'Jesus as prophetic liberator' who points to 'God's vindication of the lowly' stands in the tradition of theologians who stress the task of theology as prophecy. She could however be criticised for suggesting that it is possible to arrive at an understanding of Jesus' message by 'stripping off' its cultural context. Theological understanding is affected by both the context of the contemporary theologian, and the context of the gospels.

The practical consequences of theology as prophecy which Ruether explores recognise the importance of a vision which affirms the value of human beings and stresses the importance of mutual support, equality, participation and harmony. But she is realistic about the difficulties of making such an alternative vision concrete, since its enactment depends on the realities of political power, when she states:

> The powers and principalities are still very much in control of most of the world. The nucleus of the alternative world remains, like the Church, harbingers and experimenters with new human possibilities within the womb of the old.[44]

Work and Self-Denial

Self-negation has been recognised by feminists as a key problem for women. The kind of caring work many women perform leaves them unable to consider their own needs.[45]

Whilst for some women, the experience of paid employment undoubtedly increases their sense of autonomy and self worth, for many others the experience may reinforce their sense of self-negation. This essay has given a number of examples of the ways in which work may do so—for example a through inequality of opportunity, low pay, or adverse working conditions. Just as this is often true of paid employment, so too can it be true of domestic work at home.

Mary Grey extends an understanding of the lack of self-worth to explore the ways in which suffering and redemption in the Christian tradition, may inappropriately extend an ethic of self-sacrifice, into one in which women may be both the victims of social injustice, and also held to be responsible for it:

> The lasting effect on women is that they have been allowed to assume responsibility for suffering and injustice; when confronted by the Christian cross, women have so absorbed the ethic of self-sacrifice and the rightfulness of their being punished that they assumed their rightful place was just there on the cross with Jesus![46]

Grey's concern is to discover an understanding of Christian suffering and redemption which sets women free from being blamed as victims of injustice. Drawing on the work of the theologian Isobel Carter Heywood she argues that feminist understandings of redemption might be developed from understandings of mutuality and justice in relationships.

This understanding is based on seeing God as 'power in relation' —who works towards reciprocal relationships between God and human beings, and human beings with each other. Redemption— as a feature of God's activity in the world re-established mutuality and justice within these relationships and encompasses both the personal and political dimensions of life.

Rosemary Ruether likewise considers men to be the victims of social injustice, and redemption as a process which sets them free and transforms understandings of social power:

> Redeemed humankind can only be liberated when the victims have been empowered to be persons, and power itself has been redeemed and transformed.[47]

The paradox of some caring work which women do, is that it takes place in a social and economic context which renders many of them 'social victims'. In this context feminist theologians would argue that a contemporary understanding of redemption needs to take seriously the ways in which changes may set them more free to reach their full potential as human beings made in God's image.

Work and Service

Service ethic which emphasises refusal to complain, and accepts any personal cost as suffering for Christ's sake, leaves unjust working conditions unchallenged. Unless love for others includes a concern for justice, the ethic is service is used to legitimise oppression and maintain an unjust status quo.

Understandings of the work which women do, are often characterised by the term 'service'. Many women work for example in the 'service industries', and much work they do—for example in catering, or in caring occupations, both domestically and industrially can also be described this way. Likewise understandings of 'service' predominate in the retail trade—and area which characteristically employs large numbers of women often part-time.

However if understandings of such service are individualised and taken out of a social context, the 'service ethic', which Anne Borrowdale describes may well be misused. Understandings of service are often implicitly linked to assumptions about gender and may well reinforce assumptions that women find their greatest fulfilment in serving others.

Thus service also take place in the context of social relationship Rosemary Ruether explores this in the context of ways it has been interpreted by the church, argues that Biblical models of service were not already recommended to those who were already slaves, and thus need to be seen in the context of power and relationship

Ruether further extends her discussion to explore the ways in which symbolic understandings of Christ as servant, and encouraged his disciples to do likewise, need to be seen in the context of what service exists for:

If Christ represents this emptying out of God into service then he too cannot be seen as lord who established the lordship of some people over other people ... Jesus pours the power of the Holy Spirit back into the creation to bring about a community of love.[49]

This understanding of a community of love is further developed by Ruether in terms of the ways in which it affirms the dignity of those who have previously been servants themselves; and in the context of her understanding of women's relationships with men, she argues that such communities should reflect mutuality and reciprocity of relationship.

In the context of the work which many women do, both in terms of their domestic work and within the service industries, Anne Borrowdale argues that the important of freely making sacrifices for others is an important part of human fulfilment, but has often been carried out by women at the expense of developing this potential in men. Further in linking such an understanding to that of stereotyped notions of 'femininity' this fails to take account of the ways in which women are unique human beings:

> The loving work of women is something society cannot do without. But we need to be clearer about the meaning of love and service and to acknowledge that women are ... complex, unique and very different from each other.[50]

Work, Change and the Future

Christa Springe comments, that the way in which much women's work is organised, decreases a sense of their solidarity with each other. In exploring how multi-national companies employ young women, and aspects of black women's working lives in Britain, this essay has illustrated some of the fragmentation created by international economic relationships.[51]

The ironical example given at the end of the discussion on race and gender illustrates how religious belief and practice had been used to stabilise the working practices of some major companies. Religious believing can thus either serve to re-inforce traditional understandings of gender, or thus can be seen as a force for change. Feminist theologians challenge the ways in which gender stereotyping has affected the ways in which theology has maintained such understandings, and reflected a broken relationship between women and men. Some would claim along with Rosemary Ruether that:

The most basic expression of human community, the I – thou relationship as the relationship of men and women has victimised one half of the human race and turned the other half into tyrants.[52]

However, Ruether's argument needs to recognise the complexity of ways in which 'victimisation' and 'oppression' are manifested in the labour market, and does not fully take account of the ways in which international forces may render some more vulnerable than others. The conditions under which some women work are doubtless more favourable than others.

Letty Russell sets understandings of women's 'journey towards freedom' in a wider context of the whole of creation. She recognises that such understandings of freedom from oppression are highly contextualised, and thus underlines the importance of a sense of 'solidarity' about human liberation. Thus discovering liberation for women is to be found in process, which is achieved with others. For her:

Freedom is a journey with others and for others towards God's future.[53]

If moving towards God's future is part of the purpose of working life, several of the statements which women made about a 'better future' for their children reflect attitudes in keeping with what Charlotte Perkins Gilmore terms as a 'birth based' rather than 'death based' world view. Although her understandings may be somewhat stark, they argue that 'birth based' (female) forms of religious believing focus on the survival of future generations, rather than positing a 'death based' belief which focuses on the possible survival of individuals after their death.

Rosemary Ruether and Letty Russell both endorse a view of theology which understands change as one of its central purposes. Both however are realistic about the dangers of simplistically equating understandings of change as something to be realised in this generation, but rather one which involves human aspirations for future generations. As Ruether comments:

Our responsibility is to use our temporal life span to create a good and just future for ourselves and for our children.[54]

References

1   *Divided Loyalties*, p 61.
2   *All that is unseen*, p 5.
3   op cit, p 6.
4   *Women at Work*, p 75.
5   op cit, p 75.
6   *Women and Poverty in Britain*, p 93.
7   *New Woman New Earth*, p 6.
8   Research in contemporary third world societies suggest that high infant mortality rates, and the importance of children as insurance against old age are central reasons given for the lack of acceptance of some government population control campaigns in rural areas. These two features may arguably have likewise affected attitudes to childbirth in Britain in the nineteenth century.
9   See *Women's work and the Family in Nineteenth Century Europe*, and chapter 4 of *The Economics of Women at Work* for a more extensive discussion.
10 *Divided Loyalties*, p 60.
11 op cit, p 63.
12 *Working women: A Study of Pay and Hours*, p 86.
13 See *Working Women: A Study of Pay and Hours* for a fuller discussion of the issues.
14 *Redundant Woman*, p 98.
15 op cit, p 95.
16 op cit, p 45.
17 *Waged work—A Reader*, p 55.
18 Birnaum has suggested that such a situation arose partly because the men concerned originated from an immigrant background and had fought to preserve their 'masculinity' by redefining work as skilled labour. Craft status had become identified with 'manhood' and thus its acquisition also ensured that men retained domestic authority over women.
19 *All Day Every Day*, p 46.
20 *Redundant Women*, p 77.
21 op cit, p 44.
22 *With One Voice*, p 4.
23 op cit, p 4-5.
24 op cit p 5.
25 *Daughters of Seacole*, p 18.
26 op cit, p 15.
27 op cit, p 8.
28 op cit, p 10.
29 *Enterprising Women*, p 69.

30 op cit, p 65.
31 op cit, p 66.
32 op cit, p 70.
33 op cit, p 71.
34 op cit, p 27.
35 See recommendations in the Scarman Report of 1981.
36 *A Penny a Bag*, p 52.
37 *Waged Work—A Reader*, p 73.
38 op cit, p 75.
39 op cit, p 82.
40 *A Woman's Work*, p 35.
41 *Modern Churchman*, volume XXIX, p 23-24.
42 *Sexism & God Talk*, p 137.
43 op cit, p 136.
44 op cit, p 234.
45 *A Woman's Work*, p 66.
46 *Redeeming the Dream*, p 13.
47 *Mary the Feminine Face of the Church*, p 71.
48 *A Woman's Work*, p 95.
49 *Mary the Feminine Face of the Church*, p 72.
50 *A Woman's Work*, p 95.
51 See article by Christa Springe in *Divisions of Labour* for a fuller exploration of the theme.
52 *Sexism & God Talk*, p 160.
53 *Human Liberation in a feminist perspective*, p 25.
54 *Sexism & God Talk*, p 253.

Bibliography

A Amsden (ed): *The Economics of Women at Work*, Penguin, 1980.
P Bachu and S Westwood: *Enterprising Women*, Routledge, 1988.
A Borrowdale: *A Women's Work—Changing Christian Attitudes*, SPCK, 1989.
G Cox: *Working Women—A Study of Pay & Hours*, Greater Manchester Low Pay Unit, December 1989.
A Coyle: *Redundant Women*, The Women's Press, 1984.
R Dawson: *All that is unseen*, Church House Publications, 1987.
Glendenning and Millar (eds): *Women & Poverty in Britain*, Wheatsheaf, 1987.
M Grey: *Redeeming the Dream*, SPCK, 1989.
Feminist Review (ed): *Waged Work a reader*, Virago, 1986.
Modern Churchman: vol 29, no 6, 1986.
A Phillips: *Divided Loyalties—Dilemmas of Sex & Class*, Virago, 1987.

R Ruether: *New Women New Earth*, Seabury, 1975.

R Ruether: *Mary the Feminine Face of the Church*, SCM, 1979.

R Ruether: *Sexism & God Talk*, SCM, 1985.

L Russell: *Human Liberation in a Feminine Perspective—A Theology*, Westminster Press, 1974.

S Westwood: *All Day Every Day*, Pluto, 1979.

West Yorkshire Low Pay Unit publications:

With One Voice, 1987.

Daughters of Seacole, 1989.

A Penny a Bag, 1990.

William Temple Foundation: *Divisions of Labour*, 1985.

4

Reconciling Employment with the Care of Children

BRONWEN COHEN
and YVONNE STRACHAN

Access to child care services and associated leave and working arrangements (often called work and family provision) has now become a central issue within equal opportunities policy. The United Nations Convention on the Elimination of All Forms of Discrimination against Women stipulated in 1979 that state parties should encourage the provision of necessary supporting social services to enable parents to combine family obligations with work responsibilities and participation in public life, in particular, promoting the establishment and development of child care facilities.[1]

The Equal Opportunities Commission of Great Britain noted in a 1990 policy document that:

> Women cannot enjoy equality of opportunity unless they have access to daycare facilities for their children. The complete inadequacy of current provision for both the under fives and dependent school age children is now probably one of the most important factors restricting many women's opportunities.[2]

EC Child care Recommendation

Within the European Community, the European Commission, as part of its equal opportunities action programmes, has been examining the issue of child care since 1986. In March 1992 the Council of Ministers agreed a Council Recommendation on Child care in which all member states agreed the need for a wide range of measures 'to enable men and women to reconcile their occupational and family occupations'. The Council Recommendation notes the concern of all member states that lack of provision is 'a major barrier' to women's access to and participation in the labour market as well as their hope that 'better child care services could facilitate freedom of women and mobility on the European labour market'. It asks for a wide range of measures from member states encompassing:

- services for children
- leave arrangements for parents
- making the environment, structure and organisation of work responsive to the needs of workers with children
- promoting the sharing of responsibilities for child care between women and men.[3]

Changing Needs of Families and Demand for Child Care Services

The Recommendation represents something of a milestone—it is the first ever statement of European child care policy. It reflects recognition of the importance of work and family provision both as an essential corollary to equal opportunities legislation at a domestic and European level, and in responding to the changing needs of families. Demographic changes including declining fertility rates, changing family structures and roles have contributed to strong and rising demand for child care services, and associated work and family provisions throughout Europe and the industrialised world. These trends, together with increasing awareness of children's physical and social well being and a greater understanding of the benefits of high quality pre-school services have brought heavy demands on child care services and have brought growing recognition of the importance of finding better ways of reconciling employment with the care of children.

Fig 1:   Employment Rates of Women with a Child aged 0-9, Scotland, UK, EC1988

	Employed f/time (%)	Employed p/time	Total
Scotland	12.5	27.6	40.0
UK	13.4	32.1	45.6
EC	26.45	17.92	44.37

Scotland has not been immune from these trends. As shown in Figure 1, in 1988 40% of Scottish mothers with a child under 10 were in paid employment with a further 11% seeking employment. Surveys show that many more mothers would like to be in employment or would wish to undertake education and training if child care were available to meet their needs and which they could afford. In Scotland a 1988 survey[4] carried out by Strathclyde Regional Council found that of those mothers of under fives who were not working under a quarter would choose to stay at home if suitable child care were available and two surveys carried out in 1990 by the Scottish Child and Family Alliance[5] found that demand in some rural communities is higher than the UK average.

Child Care Services in Scotland

Demand for child care has never been higher. But services which meet the specific requirements of daycare both for pre-school and school-age children, required in particular by parents in paid employment, education and training are in extremely short supply.

In 1990, services specifically concerned with providing daycare *ie* day nurseries and childminders were only available to less than 8% of Scottish under fives. This is a generous estimate as it includes many local authority day nurseries and family centres which no longer provide daycare. Other services providing education and play are more readily available for 3 and 4 year olds. In 1990 34% of Scottish 3 and 4 year olds were in nursery education, a further 7% were in primary schools and playgroups provided places for 34% of 3 and 4 year olds. However, these services can only partially contribute to the care requirements of their parents—nursery education is predominantly part-time and playgroups are usually only open for two or three hours a week. Daycare places for school age child care (*ie*, out of school hours or in the school holidays) are very limited. A 1988 survey found there were places in Scotland for less than 0.5% of primary school children.[6]

Fig 2: Local Authority Services for Under Fives, Scotland, 1990

'Pupils under five and pupils aged five, six or more
(Source: *Scotland's Family Today*, SCAFA, 1992)

	LA DAY NURSERIES AND FAMILY CENTRES		PLAYGROUPS (LA)		LEA NURSERY SCHOOLS AND CLASSES			UNDER-FIVES IN LEA PRIMARY SCHOOLS		
	No. of places	No. of places per 1000 of pop. aged 0-4	No. of places	Places per 1000 pop. aged 0-4	F/time pupils	P/time pupils	Total*	Pupils as % of pop. aged 3 & 4	F/time pupils	Pupils as % of pop. aged 3 & 4
Borders	88	14.9	0	0.0	1	485	486	20.1	200	8.3
Central	383	23.1	0	0.0	8	2574	2762	41.9	499	7.6
Dumfries & Galloway	58	6.6	0	0.0	3	637	640	18.1	294	8.3
Fife	255	11.3	24	1.1	151	4402	4553	49.4	699	7.6
Grampian	279	8.8	0	0.0	265	3172	3437	26.5	860	6.6
Highland	29	2.2	0	0.0	1	735	736	13.7	380	7.1
Lothian	745	15.9	70	1.5	854	7680	8534	46.3	1157	6.3
Strathclyde	2720	18.0	157	1.0	1213	17971	19184	31.4	4793	7.8
Tayside	690	29.2	0	0.0	431	2974	3405	35.0	559	5.8
Orkney	0	0.0	0	0.0	0	106	106	21.2	27	5.4
Shetland	0	0.0	0	0.0	0	138	138	20.7	41	6.1
Western Isles	5	2.8	0	0.0	0	0	0	0.0	52	7.3
Scotland	5252	16.1	251	0.8	2927	41054	43981	33.5	9561	7.3

Fig 3: Private and Voluntary Services for Under Fives, Scotland, 1990

*Scottish Office estimate

(Source: *Scotland's Family Today*, SCAFA, 1992)

	PRIVATE AND VOLUNTARY DAY NUSERIES AND FAMILY CENTRES		CHILDMINDERS		PLAYGROUPS (VOLUNTARY AND PRIVATE)		INDEPENDENT SCHOOLS	
	No. of places	% per 1000 pop. aged 0-4	No. of places provided	Places per 1000 pop. aged 0-4	No. of places	Places per 1000 pop. aged 0-4	No. of P/time pupils under 5	Pupils as % of pop. aged 3 & 4
Borders			438	74.2	1396	236.6	18	0.7
Central			1126	70.0	2180	131.5	50	0.8
Dumfries & Galloway	NO		186	21.0	2080	235.3	0	0.0
Fife			1385	61.5	2443	108.5	48	0.5
Grampian	RELIABLE		1649	50.8	4986	153.6	220	1.7
Highland			563	43.1	3470	265.5	0	0.0
Lothian	INFORMATION		3026	64.7	5165	110.4	415	2.3
Strathclyde			3930	25.9	16611	110.0	638	1.0
Tayside	AVAILABLE		1572	66.5	3731	157.7	9	0.1
Orkney			82	63.9	627	488.7	0	0.0
Shetland			39	23.9	579	355.0	0	0.0
Western Isles			30	17.0	851	482.1	0	0.0
Scotland	2500*	15.8	14023	43.0	44119	135.4	1398	1.1

Access to Employment Provisions

Scottish parents also miss out on some of the employment provisions which have been developing in many other European countries. Many women do not have access to maternity leave or maternity pay because of the restrictive qualifying requirements. Recent survey evidence found that 40% of employed UK pregnant women fail to qualify for the right to return to work following childbirth rising to over half of semi-skilled and unskilled manual workers.[7] Only a handful of employers throughout the whole of the UK offer parental (child care) leave. Fathers have no access to any statutory form of leave provision in this country and access to family leave for either parent is extremely variable.

Impact of Inadequacies in Work and Family Provision

The impact of inadequate provision—both services and employment entitlements—upon women is considerable. Absence of child care prevents a large number of women from working and affects the hours and nature of the employment of many others. The overwhelming majority of women with a child under 10 work part-time, sometimes through choice, sometimes through lack of child care and frequently with consequences for their pay and employment opportunities. Part-time work is often only available in certain types of occupations, frequently low paid and reinforcing gender segregation within employment. Part-time employees may be excluded from additional benefits in the workplace such as pensions, share options or bonuses, do not have the same access to employment protection as full-time employees and in general have few opportunities for training and promotion.

Research evidence has shown that childbearing and childrearing substantially reduce employment experience and earnings potential and costs the average UK mother of two more than half her potential lifetime's earnings.[8] The heavy price that women themselves pay rebounds also on their families, contributing to the high levels of child poverty in this country. A recent estimate suggests that over 440,000 (38%) of children under the age of 18 are living in households with below 50% of average income—a commonly used poverty measure—and that this includes more than 135,000 (42%) of under fives.[9] This compares with 26% of children in the UK including an estimated 32% of under fives.[10] The higher proportion of under fives reflects the lower employment rates for mothers of children in this age group. Children living in poverty are more likely to be living in a household where the mother does not work. This is true of two parent families and is also true of lone parent families although these are more likely than other families to be living in poverty even when the parent is in paid employment. Employment rates of UK lone mothers are low and particularly so in the case of full-time employment—only 6% of lone mothers are in full-time employment, the lowest rate in the European community.[11]

Heavy Use of Informal and ad hoc Child Care Arrangements

Children are affected in other ways. The daycare shortfall means that they are frequently cared for through a multiplicity of arrangements which may be unsatisfactory to both parents and children. The most frequently used form of child care is care by relatives. The 1981 Women and Employment Survey found that 50% of British women working part-time and 13% working full-time used husbands to care for their children.[12] A large number of women working part-time do so in the evenings or nights when their spouses/partners are available to provide care and arrangements such as this can put considerable strain upon families. Other relatives used to provide child care are grandmothers, aunts, uncles, and older brothers and sisters. In the Scottish Low Pay unit's 1991 survey, 42% of respondents relied on the children's grandparents for care and 15% used other relatives. A further one in five had reciprocal arrangements with friends and neighbours and 10% used unregistered childminders. The majority of respondents (61%) used only informal child care arrangements compared with 28% using only formal care.[13] Some groups experience particular difficulties in obtaining access for formal services. For example, women from some black and minority ethnic groups have higher employment rates but the problems they may encounter from institutional and individual racism can make it more difficult for them to obtain access to suitable high quality provision, reinforcing in some cases their frequently weaker position in the labour market. And in Scotland's many rural areas formal daycare services are frequently non-existent.[14] The 1981 British survey found that older children accounted for 4% of arrangements for out of school care.[15]

Although parents may in some cases prefer informal arrangements the preponderance of such arrangements reflects the difficulties of parents in both finding and affording suitable child care services.

Women using formal services often pay a considerable proportion of their income to meet child care costs. The Scottish Low Pay Unit survey found that 46% of respondents were paying between 20% and 50% of their take home pay on child care. Nevertheless the overwhelming majority of them (72%) were still paying less than £40 per week. In services where subsidies are not available—and less than 2% of children under three have access to publicly funded services—the inability of parents to pay for child care contributes to low levels of pay and poor conditions of employment for child care workers and can in this way directly affect the quality of care.

The combination of having to rely on inadequate or less than satisfactory child care arrangements and/or paying low wages to childcarers can lead to feelings of guilt. This is exacerbated by the still frequently heard criticism that a mother's place is in the home.

Comparison of child Care Services in Scotland and European Community

In Scotland, both children and parents have access to far fewer services and less public support than in most other countries in the European Community.

**Fig 4:   EC Publicly Funded Child Care services
as a Percentage of all Children in Age Group**

	Children under 3	Children from 3 to compulsory school age	Age when compulsory schooling begins
Belgium	20%	95%+	6 years
Denmark	48%	85%	7 years
France	20%	95%+	6 years
Germany	3%	65-70%	6-7 years
Greece	4%	65-70%	5.5 years

Ireland	2%	55%	6 years
Italy	5%	85%+	6 years
Luxembourg	2%	55-60%	5 years
Netherlands	2%	50-55%	5 years
Portugal	6%	35%	6 years
Spain		65-70%	6 years
United Kingdom*	2%	35-40%	5 years

Source: CEC, a

* Government statistics on European comparisons commonly include playgroups within UK provision for this age group. These are not included in the EC Childcare Network comparative tables as these are based on publicly funded places providing education or care for a significant period of time. Although a substantial minority of children attend playgroups in the UK, their average attendance is only 5 hours per week (compared with, for example, 30-40 hours per week in French nursery education), and only a third of playgroups receive any public funds, with an average grant covering less than 10 per cent of running costs. Informal provision of this kind such as drop-in centres and parent and toddler groups are excluded from these comparisons.

(Source: CEC *Child care in the European Community,* 1985-90)

This is true of services for which public responsibility has been acknowledged and which are publicly provided—such as nursery education. In France and Belgium, for example, over 95% of three and four year olds are in nursery education in general full-time compared with 34% of Scottish 3 and 4 year olds for whom nursery education is in general—and increasingly—part-time.

In relation to daycare UK government policies over more than a decade have emphasised the responsibility of parents themselves to find and pay for daycare except when children and families are in particular need of provision on the grounds of welfare. For some time, successive ministers have specifically rejected the concept of public responsibility in ensuring the availability of daycare for working parents, a policy position almost unique in the European Community. UK government policy has emphasised that while the provision of daycare is not a matter of public responsibility (except for children in need) employers themselves should consider helping their employees with child care. However, survey evidence shows that employers' response so far to this policy has been very limited.

Employer Assistance with Work and Family Provision

A 1989 survey by Industrial Relations Review and Report found that only 3% of organisations surveyed provided child care facilities and a 1988/89 survey carried out by the Policy Studies Institution on behalf of the Department of Employment, the EOC and the DSS found a similar proportion of mothers reporting assistance with a workplace creche or other help with child care, representing only a small increase since a similar study carried out by the Policy Studies Institute nine years earlier.[16]

Fig 5:   Mothers' Accounts of Arrangements available to help them continue working

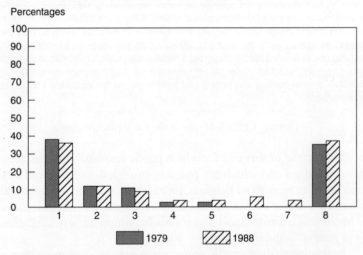

1 Part-time working opportunities
2 Flexitime or flexible working hours
3 Shiftworking
4 Workplace crèche or other help with childcare

5 Scope to work part of time at home
6 Job share scheme (not asked 1979)
7 Career break scheme (not asked 1979)
8 None of the listed arrangements

(Source: S McRae and W W Daniel:
Maternity Rights: The Experience of Women and Employers, PSI 1991)

As figure 5 shows, provisions relating to leave, part-time working, and flexibility of hours are more widely available than help with child care but are still only accessible to a minority of employees, with only a small increase in such provisions over the past decade. The most extensive form of assistance is in the form of part-time working opportunities which, as we have already noted, may assist women in returning to employment but may limit the rates of pay and access to benefits and promotional opportunities unless offered in a form such as job sharing which provides access to rates of pay and benefits on a similar basis to full-time employees. The Scottish Low Pay Unit survey found that just over a half of its respondents were allowed time off work to look after a sick child. Forty-five per cent were not allowed time off and just over a third of those who were allowed had to use their holiday entitlement. Nearly a half (48%) of all part-time workers able to take time off had to take unpaid leave.[17] Few employers have extended significantly the statutory minimum maternity provision but a proposed EC Directive on the Protection of Pregnant Women at Work (agreed in principle in 1991 but still awaiting final agreement) will widen access to maternity leave to all women in employment (with some exceptions in relation to fixed term contracts) as is currently the case in all other EC countries.

The PSI study together with other surveys has shown that public sector employers are more likely to make arrangements for both child care and other provisions than the private sector.

Fig 6: **Examples of the Contrast between the Public and Private Sectors in the Enhancement of Maternity Rights**

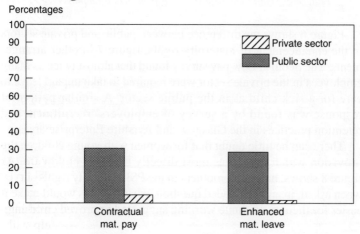

Percentages

(Source: S McRae and W W Daniel:
Maternity Rights: The Experience of Women and Employers, PSI 1991)

Fig 7:   Differences between the Public and Private Sectors in Arrangements to help Mothers of Young Children

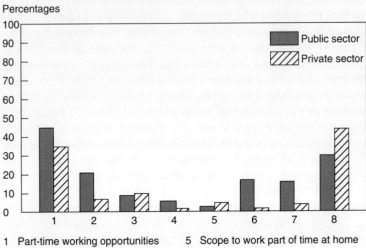

Percentages

1 Part-time working opportunities
2 Flexitime or flexible working hours
3 Shiftworking
4 Workplace crèche or other help with childcare

5 Scope to work part of time at home
6 Job share scheme
7 Career break scheme
8 None of the listed arrangements

(Source: S McRae and W W Daniel:
Maternity Rights: The Experience of Women and Employers, PSI 1991)

Figure 6 shows the difference between public and private sectors in the enhancement of maternity rights, figure 7 in other arrangements. The Scottish Low pay survey found that almost twice as many employees in the private sector were required to take unpaid leave to care for a sick child as in the public sector. A similar pattern of response was found by a survey of employers' recruitment and retention practices in the Glasgow and Ayrshire Enterprise areas.[18]

There can be little doubt that for women with young children the provision which is seen as most directly useful is child care. As figure 8 shows, half of all mothers in the PSI maternity rights survey when asked, in an open-ended question, what changes would make it easier for them to continue working suggested improved child care.

Fig 8:   Changes sought by Mothers to make it easier to continue working after a Baby

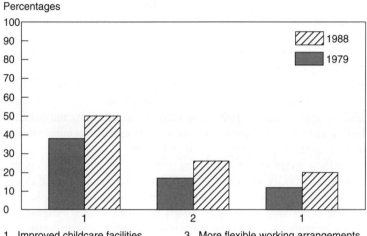

1 Improved childcare facilities   3 More flexible working arrangements
2 Improved maternity rights

(Source: S McRae and W W Daniel:
Maternity Rights: The Experience of Women and Employers, PSI 1991)

The evidence suggest that very few employers see themselves as in a position to adequately respond to these child care needs. In Scotland single employer workplace nurseries are extremely rare and very few employers offer any assistance with child care costs. A number of schemes involving the payment of child care 'cheques' or vouchers (like luncheon vouchers) have developed but have not been taken up to any significant extent. The reasons for this include the taxing of employees on such vouchers. Further disadvantages from an employer's perspective include the possibility that such payments may inflate the costs of child care without contributing to increased availability in particular of these services preferred by parents.

A more promising child care model for many employers is that of co-operating with other employers, organisations and local authorities in nurseries and out of school facilities on a 'partnership' basis. One example of this model is the Partnership in Child care scheme developed by Fife Regional Council which involves the establishment of five partnership nurseries offering places to local employers. Fife Regional Council has received funds for this project from the

EC Regional Development Fund and from the Europe Social Fund. A further Scottish project is that which is initiated by the Scottish Development Agency and latterly developed by the Glasgow Development Agency. This began as a nursery partnership including local authorities (no longer specifically included) and now involves the Glasgow Development Agency, Scottish Enterprise, BBC and National Savings Bank although it is hoped to involve other employers as the schemes develop. The project envisages a network of four nurseries within Glasgow offering 160 places and it is hoped that it will be operational by 1993. The project, approved by the Scottish Office aims to assist businesses in attracting and retaining staff in order to address problems of skill shortages.

In these examples, the initiating party was a development agency and local authority. But the partnership proposal has been used extensively in the Midlands Bank's nursery programme for its employees.

The partnership model, particularly where it involves local authorities overcomes some of the difficulties associated with setting up single employer nurseries, can assist the viability and cost effectiveness of services within a community and avoid a pattern of services which provides separately for children of employed parents.

It would seem improbable that the child care needs of Scottish employees will ever be adequately met by employers alone. And while employers are more involved in offering leave provisions and some flexibility in hours, it also seems evident that a statutory framework is required for such provision. If approved, a number of EC initiatives in this area would considerably assist many employees. These include (in addition to the Directive on the Protection of Pregnant Women at Work) proposals to improve employment conditions for part-time workers and to provide all male and female employees with a minimum entitlement to parental or child care leave.

But is is also clear that there is considerable room for initiatives by both employers and trade unions—as envisaged by the EC recommendation on Child care which calls for action not only by member states but also by employers and trade unions and other relevant organisations and individuals. In relation to child care there are certainly possibilities for larger employers to effectively meet the child care needs of their own employees and somewhat wider possibilities to initiate and contribute to partnership schemes with other employers, voluntary agencies and with local authorities and development agencies.

There is a pressing need for employers to reconsider their leave provision, working hours and working practices from a perspective which allows consideration for the requirements of employees with children—and indeed other family commitments. Integral to any such review has to be an awareness that while the absence of work and family provision is at the heart of the problem confronting many women, developments of provision and any reviews of practices have to take account of the needs to promote a greater sharing of the care of children and other family responsibilities between men and women —the fourth area of action envisaged by the EC Recommendation. Organisational policies which, for example, provide career breaks for women employees whilst tacitly encouraging ever increasing working hours for fathers of young children cannot be regarded as conducive to good equal opportunities practice. It is worth noting in this context that Scottish fathers of under fives (like other fathers in the UK) work the longest hours in Europe. In 1988, 35% of fathers with a child aged under five worked fifty hours a week or more; two thirds of mothers of under fives worked fewer than thirty hours per week.[19] Other areas for examination include requirements and out of hours meetings called at short notice.

The Role of Trade Unions

Trade Unions have an important role to play in encouraging a re-examination of provisions and work place practices. The role of trade unions has been of considerable importance in developing equality bargaining agendas within the workplace. The Strathclyde University survey of Glasgow and Ayrshire Enterprise areas showed that trade unions can have an impact in raising issues such as equal opportunities and flexible working arrangements. Many unions have begun providing negotiating materials on child care as well as information on maternity rights and specific education courses and shop stewards training in equality bargaining are being undertaken by many unions. Ways of improving women's representation on decision making and negotiating bodies are also being examined. This is being assisted by the process of reorganisation that is being undertaken by many trade unions. For example the NALGO/NUPE/COHSE merger will result in proportional representation at all levels for women and the TGWU is conducting a full consultation on measure to improve women's representation.

Developments such as they may be expected to strengthen union commitment to work and family initiatives within employer/union negotiations. Further possibilities for action by unions—in particular those representing child care workers—are suggested by some examples of initiatives by Danish trade unions. One such example is that of an innovation fund set up by the BUPL (Danish Union of Trained Childcare Workers). The fund dispenses one million kroner each year for innovative projects and research. Another example is that of the organisation, Dansoc Systems, established with capital from the pension funds of the child care trade union and with the support of the Danish Ministry of Social Affairs and local authorities to advise on the planning and establishment of daycare services on a Europe-wide basis.

Understanding by both employers and trade unions of the issues relating to reconciling employment with the care of children is becoming vital not only in improving provisions such as child care and leave entitlements but also in responding to changing structures and patterns of employment. This may involve alleviating the impact of streamlining and rationalisation on work patterns which have evolved in the past in relation to women with children. A recent example of this for one Scottish union has been a factory with three shift working in which the part-time shift was used by those predominantly caring for children. In the moves to achieve a reduction in the working week the only solution which met both the demand of the predominantly female workforce for the hour to be taken off the end of the week and the management criteria of no loss of production was to increase the hours of the part-time shift. Although the part-time shift received enhanced payments, there was a recognition that the reduction in the working week had come at its expense. Part-time workers with children were assisted by the Union to reorganise their child care arrangements and all managed to resolve their problems although not without difficulty in some cases.

Conclusion

The European Community Recommendation on child care makes clear that the achievement of reconciliation of child care and employment is a shared responsibility. It asks for action from governments at national, regional and local levels, from employers and trade unions as well as other relevant organisations.

WORK AND FAMILY CHECKLIST

Review workplace practices and requirements from a work and family perspective

Examine rates of return from maternity leave and child related reasons for employees leaving or changing jobs/working hours

* Review leave provisions and working arrangements
  - pregnancy and maternity
  - paternity leave
  - parental and family leave
  - career breaks
  - job sharing and flexible working arrangements
* Survey employee child care needs
* Examine and develop child care options
  - workplace nurseries
  - developing day nurseries in partnership with others
  - child care allowances/vouchers
  - helping employees to find child care
* Develop a corporate work and family policy

In this country it is evident that we need a strengthened legislative framework and substantially increased public resourcing of both child care services and leave provision. Action by government at both a national and local level is essential if families are to receive the assistance they require. But this should not be allowed to conceal the responsibility of others and the many initiatives which can be taken in the workplace now by both employers and trade unions.

References

1 UN Convention, Articles 112(c), 18(3).
2 *The Key to Real Choice and Action, Plan for Child care*, EOC, Manchester, 1990.

3   Council Recommendation on Child care, EC 31/3/92.

4   G Scott: *Families Under Five in Strathclyde*, Strathclyde Regional Council, 1989.

5   *Child care in Rural Communities—Scotland in Europe*, HMSO, SCAFA/Borders Regional Council, 1991, Family Matters.

6   *Kids Clubs Network: A Patchwork of Provision*, KCN, 1998.

7   S McRae, S and W W Daniel: *Maternity Rights and the Experience of Women and Employers*, PSI, London, 1991.

8   H Joshi, H1987, in C Glendinning and J Millar: *The Cost of Caring: Women and Poverty in Britain*, Wheatsheaf, Brighton. See Joshi, H1992, CEPR.

9   *Scotland's Families Today*, SCAFA, 1992.

10 Cohen and Fraser: *Child care in a Modern Welfare State*, IPPR, 1991.

11 *Scotland's Families Today*, SCAFA, 1992.

12 J Martin and Roberts: *Women and Employment: A Lifetime Perspective*, HMSO, 1984.

13 V Brown, V and L Tait: *Working Miracles: Experiences of Jobs and Child care*, Scottish Low Pay Unit, 1992).

14 SCAFA, 1991.

15 Martin and Roberts: op. cit.

16 S McRae and W W Daniel: op.cit. See figure 5.

17 Brown and Tait: op. cit.

18 M Steel *et al*: *Employers Retention and Recruitment practices*: *Glasgow/Ayrshire Enterprise Areas*, Strathclyde University Research Development Fund, 1991.

19 Cohen: *Caring for Children*, Report, Family Policy Studies Centre, 1990.

5

Getting to the Top

An Uphill Struggle for Women in Scotland

LESLEY HART

This chapter has as its origins in work carried out by a colleague, Elisabeth Gerver, and myself during 1989 and 1990 on the topic of women and decision making in Scotland. We were aware that for a number of years girls in Scotland have been leaving school more highly qualified than their brothers and indeed are well represented in further and higher education courses. There seemed to us however to be strikingly few women employed in senior positions in Scotland. In 1989 indeed women in senior positions in any professional group could be counted on one hand or no hands at all. Of the 72 Scottish Members of Parliament, 3 were female. No Regional or Islands Council had a female chief executive. Of the 24 individuals in the top 3 tiers of the Scottish civil service, 23 were male. In one of the major Scottish banks, only 1% of branch managers was female and all the senior executives were male. Only 5% of the entries in the 1988-89 edition of *Who's Who in Scotland* were of females. Overall, participation by women in senior positions in Scotland tended to hover between 0 and 5%. This proportion appeared to hold true regardless of the proportion of women entrants to particular professions.

More will be said about future trends at the end of this chapter but the most recent statistics available do not show marked increases in the numbers of women in top positions. In the 1992 General Election the number of female MPs in Scotland rose to five. In some professions, however, *eg* teaching the percentage of women headteachers, deputy headteachers and assistant headteachers in Scotland has fallen slightly.

Current figures show that women are becoming increasingly well represented at lower levels in most professional and managerial employment in Scotland but that they are still present in very small numbers in senior positions and scarcely ever at the very top. This pattern seems to be a much more extreme variant of a common pattern elsewhere in the UK and in other European countries.

In order to find put why this is so we interviewed 50 women in senior and/or influential positions in different professional groupings including government, education, law, medicine, industry, finance, voluntary organisations, the media and the church. We defined senior positions as being the top 3 or 4 levels of decision making in institutions or organisations.

The resulting study was published in 1991 as *Strategic Women: how do they manage in Scotland?*, and in this chapter, I would like to highlight some of its findings.

Survivors' Views

The fifty women interviewed have survived and indeed flourished in their professional lives in Scotland. Although they may be unrepresentative of women as a whole in Scotland the interviewees have been for many years in positions in which they could assess at first hand the attitudes of a wide range of both men and women towards living and working in Scotland. So how far did they feel that Scotland has offered them—and other women—a favourable environment in which to develop their careers? Some views were positive:

> Scotland is a good place for women to work. Scots generally are individualistic, and this helps women, who also can do well on an individual basis.

But for every positive comment about Scotland there were many negative ones, particularly from women who had lived and worked in other countries.

> In Scotland attitudes are definitely gender skewed. From talking to and working with men in Scotland, I've found that very often they are either suspicious of women or contemptuous of them.

> There are probably not as many opportunities [for women] in Scotland as in England or other European Countries ... I travel around Europe and I see many more women in senior positions in other countries.

There was even an east–west divide identified by the interviewees

The west of Scotland is very entrenched about the role of women; things are especially difficult there.

There is a much more macho image in the west of Scotland.

Factors in Female Under-representation

There are a number of significant social, political and economic traditions which have affected the types and levels of jobs undertaken by women in Scotland. In fact, for most of the twentieth century in Scotland the prevailing social attitude has been that a woman's place is in the home. Even during the 1950s and 60s the economic activity rate of married women in Scotland was only about two thirds of the British average. The rate of female activity only began to catch up with the rest of Britain in the 1970s.

Politically, during the twentieth century, Scotland has always been strongly socialist with the prevailing rhetoric of socialism in Scotland emphasising class struggle rather than gender issues.

During the nineteenth century and the first half of the twentieth century the heavy industries of engineering, shipbuilding and coal mining traditionally employed men rather than women.

Since the 1970s major changes have been occurring. Evidence shows that social attitudes about women's paid employment are changing. Men's expectations about women's employment are becoming more positive and less restrictive, although men's attitudes remain more restrictive than women's. The economic activity rates of women in Scotland have increased substantially largely due to the expansion in the service sector and now exceed the British average.

But if some traditions and cultures are changing in Scotland making it easier and more acceptable for women to work, there are still others which hold women back from progressing in their career. Among those cited by the interviewees are:

(i)   Informal Selection Methods which use Old Boys Networks

As one interviewee said:

It's very significant that there are so few women at senior level in Scotland. Like goes for like. Job descriptions are very often drawn up with a particular person—who just happens to be male—in mind.

The fact that many women seem to remain at middle management level was explained by another interviewee who suggested that

> There is a myth—kept going by men—that the top is always harder

(ii)   Attitudes of Men

Men's attitudes towards working with women who are at a senior level seem to fall into two main categories

> First there are those who treat women as their equals and who judge their female colleagues purely on their professional competence. There seemed to be broad agreement that particular professional fields—notably law and computing—may now offer genuinely equal opportunities to women

> There is no real discrimination in my profession. At the end of the day it comes down to the ability, especially as an advocate. You are only as good as your last case. Whether you are male or female is irrelevant.

> But the attitudes of many men, especially older men, are still quite negative. The concept of women working may have been accepted but they still seem to have problems in accepting women as their peers or as their superiors

Comments from our interviewees included:

> Men are quite often frightened of women, especially intelligent women. Men like being in herds; they like everyone being the same.

> Most men would prefer to work with other men.

> Many men find it hard to relate to a female boss.

In many organisations in Scotland gender is still not seen as an issue and where there is no issue there cannot be a problem, far less a solution!

(iii)   Attitudes of Women

While acknowledging that it is typically more difficult for women to reach senior positions, most of the interviewees tended however to believe that women as well as men are implicated in the fact that there are relatively small numbers of women in senior positions:

> A major cause of there being so few women in senior positions is women's cultural background, which leads them to very low career aspirations.

> Women have to be much more determined and need the extra dimension which I regret to say is not always there with women.

> Women tend to underestimate their abilities.

Specific Constrains and Conflicts faced by Career Women in Scotland

In addition to the numerous attitudinal and cultural factors, the interviewees identified several other constrains and conflicts with which they themselves had been faced. Three main ones were:

(i) Domestic Commitments

The major areas of domestic responsibilities which affected all the interviewees to a greater or lesser extent were: housework, the care of the elderly and child care.

Whether married or single, nearly all of the interviewees undertook a substantial amount of responsibility for housework. As might be expected from national UK findings (see, for example, *Social Trends*, 1989), the married interviewees tended to report that husbands provide more substantial verbal than practical support, with more male attention being given to child care than to housework.

The single interviewees with children found, understandably, the greatest difficulty in getting sufficient help with housework, at least while children were young. Although such households may have a lower income than the normally two income households of married interviewees, the interviewees who were single mothers reported a particularly high use of employed domestic help while their children were young.

As *Social Trends* (1989) shows, even in households where the woman worked full-time outside the home, household tasks are not shared equally: where both partners work full-time, in 72% of households housework is still done mainly by women; it is shared equally only in 22%. In practice, then, the domestic lives of married women who are employed full-time in Scotland remains much more demanding than those of married men. This circumstance in itself is likely to create disadvantages for women who aspire to senior positions.

(ii)   Elderly Relatives

A second important demand in the domestic lives of some of the interviewees was the need to care for elderly relatives, either at home or by frequent visits. It appeared that such responsibilities were assumed willingly and fully by both married and single interviewees, although those who cared for elderly relatives commented on the time and often the stress involved in doing so. Because the interviewees worked, or have worked, predominantly full-time, however, none of the interviews cared full-time for an elderly relative.

At a time when the numbers of old people in the community are increasing rapidly, the interviewees did not share the particularly difficult circumstances of those who provided such caring full-time. The very fact of their not sharing these circumstances, however, raised a number of questions about those women who have not been able to undertake full-time employment or to embark on serious careers because of their responsibility for elderly relatives.

(iii)   Children

By far the most significant domestic issue in the lives of just under half of the interviewees, however, was that of children. There was considerable doubt amongst the interviews about whether it was possible to resolve an apparently irreconcilable conflict between providing good quality child care and having a serious career. It was primarily for this reason that many of the married interviewees had deliberately chosen to remain childless. The difficulties of combining children and a serious career may also be reflected in the fact that those of the interviewees who are parents had also chosen very diverse ways of trying to combine both. To begin with, the variable in which the interviewees who were mothers were most unlike one another was that of child care, where substantial numbers had chosen variously, full-time career breaks, part-time career breaks or continuous full-time employment.

The findings suggested that there is, indeed, a good chance that a conflict between young children and careers may be almost irreconcilable—given the present low level of provision of good quality, affordable child care in Scotland.

It is thus not surprising that more than half of the sample was childless. But it remains a matter for serious long-term concern that such a high proportion of able women are choosing not to bear children because of the particular conflict created by the present level of provision of child care in Britain. The lack of affordable high quality child care is also likely to be a major—if not even the major—factor in the lives of almost all mothers who decide that they would like to re-enter the labour market.

Those mothers for whom private child care is too expensive tend to work part-time. The United Kingdom has one of the lowest proportions of publicly funded child care and the highest proportion of female part-time workers in the European Community. The problem is that part-time jobs tend to have both low pay and low status, unlikely to lead to more substantial employment, much less to serious career development.

Despite the difficulties, the overwhelming fact remains that those of the interviewees who did decide to become mothers expressed primarily delight and joy in their, and, as far as we could tell, the children themselves appear to thrive. Moreover, the intriguing fact remains that, even where they had taken (usually brief) full-time career breaks, the mothers in the interviewees did not otherwise appear to have careers which were significantly different from other senior women. Such women are, in themselves proof that children can be combined with serious careers, but their paucity is also an indication of the sometimes extreme difficulty of doing so.

Partners Geographical Mobility

By far the largest proportion of those of the interviewees who were or are married reported leaving their initial or an early job to follow their husband's career moves. The pattern is especially characteristic of those women who took career breaks or worked part-time after the birth of their children:

> I always thought I would get married, and I did so when I was twenty-five, by which time I had already worked for five years after graduation. My husband [a university lecturer] and we went straight to the United States after we were married. I worked professionally there. When we returned I worked part-time professionally until the birth of our first child. Then we moved to [England], and I returned to study part-time, doing an external degree. When we returned to Scotland, I worked part-time professionally.

There are candid acknowledgments of the mobility problems created by marriage:

> By and large my marriages have helped my career. But if I were single I would be much more mobile. This could be a problem in the future if I want promotion.

> I was working in a job I loved in London when I got married. My husband didn't want to move to London, so we agreed that I would apply for jobs in Glasgow. But if I had been free my preference would have been to move to another job in London.

The pattern of both partners moving to accommodate male jobs, however, seems to be changing. A number of the interviewees commented on ways in which families have taken account of the career needs of both partners. In a very few instances, neither husband nor wife wanted to move from the part of Scotland where they now lived, so mobility was not in itself a problem. Some professional couples have agreed to part-time dual site marriages as the only solution to the geographically conflicting demands of their careers:

> When my husband moved to [England], his firm said that they could find work for me and asked what I did and how much I earned. When he told them, they quickly changed their mind. Now he works in [England] and I work in Scotland; we meet at weekends.

Sex Discrimination and UK Legislation

There is widespread agreement amongst both sexes that women generally have to be more able and to work harder than men to reach the same level of career development. This perception is also expressed by many of the interviewees across nearly the full range of professions and areas of work which they represented. There were also many stories about straight forward sex discrimination

> I stayed in my first job for three years. The career prospects in the company were not nearly as good as I had hoped, largely because I was a woman. It was a very chauvinistic company. There was only one other female ... and it was clear from the outset that neither of us was going to be promoted to any high level of responsibility. The manager for whom I worked didn't hide his chauvinism. He, for example, sent his daughter to a state school while sending his son to a fee-paying school. It wasn't, so he kept telling me, worth paying out money just to educate a girl.

> There are still barriers in society—they're called men. More and more women are becoming attracted to self-employment and, indeed, are being successful at setting up their own business. But there are major difficulties especially at the beginning of such an enterprise. Very often bank managers are still prejudiced against women. It's a great problem for many women to get financial backing for their business.

So how did the interviewees deal with sex discrimination? Overwhelmingly, they deliberately had not sought the legal redress available:

> I've heard through feedback from interviews in two different institutions that there was sex discrimination against me on the part of the largely or entirely male appointments committees. On another occasion, I strongly suspected that my male head of department ensured that I would not be promoted within his department. But in none of these cases did I ever seriously consider going to a tribunal. Any case would be very difficult, consisting largely of hearsay. More importantly for me, it would have been professional suicide to take such institutions to a tribunal. But

I've always felt guilty that, by not taking the cases to a tribunal, I have not helped other women as much as I should.

Fairer and more effective equal opportunities provision was identified by the interviewees many of whom believed that legislation should be strengthened:

I am a firm believer in legislation. The problem about the ineffectiveness of much current equal opportunities is that the need to prove each case of sex discrimination rather than have class actions means that most cases just don't get brought forward in the first place. I'm especially hopeful about the impact which I hope the European Community will have on our equal opportunities legislation in the future.

More and better sex discrimination legislation should be brought in. Legislation, I believe very strongly, does change attitudes.

Given the above picture of problems and barriers apparently facing women who wish to progress their career in Scotland it is not surprising perhaps that so few women do make it to the top. Those who do are, in fact, remarkably like each other in many ways especially in their strong positive personalities. It is interesting to note that very rarely were words like 'problems' and 'barriers' mentioned by these women but rather 'challenges' and 'constraints'.

Key Factors to Success

Interviewees' early experiences at home appeared to have laid the foundation for later achievement in professional life. Interviews' family backgrounds were characterised by:

- early development of organising abilities
- mothers who worked outside the home in paid or voluntary employment
- commitment to religious or political causes

Above all, most of the interviewees' families placed substantial emphasis on education and the achievement of academic qualifications. This strategy appears to have been particularly important in shaping interviewees' high level of participation in both higher education and continuing professional education.

As they moved into paid employment, interviewees' career strategies had much in common with each other and included:

- tapestried careers, creating a pattern from related areas of work
- emphasis on innovation and change, including a tendency to make major career moves every four to seven years
- hard work, usually over long hours

In combining their personal and professional lives, too, the interviewees shared many similar characteristics:

- belief in the need for balance
- high level of awareness of the difficulty of combining a serious career with the care of young children
- commitment to a high level of activity in a wide range of leisure interests and voluntary work

Overall, perhaps the most crucial factor, which appeared to run through nearly all of the interviews, was a general, realistic recognition of success as hard won, with difficult choices to be made. A number of the interviewees referred spontaneously to the need to demolish the myth of the superwoman, who has, and can do, everything.

Indicators for the Future

As mentioned at the beginning of the chapter, albeit from very small numbers, the proportions of women in major professions in Scotland grew during the 1980s and are expected to continue to grow during the 1990s. Most professional Institutes cite increased female membership, *eg* the Institute of Chartered Accountants quote a rise from 5% in 1980 to 11% in 1990. It is more difficult however, to assess how many women are reaching senior posts. In the 1990-91 edition of *Who's Who in Scotland,* the percentage of female entries has risen slightly from 5–7%, but, as pointed out at the beginning of the chapter, the numbers in the top posts in the teaching profession have fallen slightly in the last few years.

Positive Steps

In order to develop the potential of the female workforce two new initiatives have recently been launched. In 1990 'Training 2000 Scotland' was set up. This organisation is a specialist partnership for trainees and managers to provide information on the training of women on all levels, to update trainees on new approaches to staff development and training, and to establish links practitioners. It publishes a quarterly newsletter, and organises conferences, seminars and training events throughout Scotland. A recent publication produced by Training 2000 entitled *Local Enterprise Companies and Women—Releasing the Potential* has been issued to all Local Enterprise companies in Scotland.

On a UK wide basis, 'Opportunity 2000—a Business in the Community' venture was launched in the Autumn of 1991 by John Major. It has the specific aim of promoting the role of women at the top of Britain's most powerful organisations including government departments. Every organisation taking part in the initiative has to set targets for the recruitment and promotion of women within their workforces. Interest has been reasonably high amongst UK employers with several hundred now being members of the organisation. But despite the two above initiatives it has been interesting to note that women's issues were noticeable by their absence during the 1992 general election campaign. It is indeed doubtful according to the Equal Opportunities Commission if any political party has yet developed a coherent strategy on equal opportunities.

The Future

Our study concluded that women in Scotland can, indeed, make it to the top but that the road they have to follow may well be long and uphill and is certainly not for the faint hearted. This chapter thus ends in a mood of cautious optimism and in the hope that initiatives such as Training 2000 and Opportunity 2000 will be successful in their aim to develop the undoubted career potential of women in Scotland.

References

Gerver, Elisabeth and Lesley Hart: *Strategic Women: How do they manage in Scotland?*, Aberdeen University Press, 1991.

Social Trends 19, Her Majesty's Stationery Office, 1989.

Who's Who in Scotland, Carrick Publishing, 1988, 1990.

Part II

The Root
of the Trouble

6

Sex and Sexism
in the Workplace*

ANNE BORROWDALE

[*With acknowledgment to SPCK for permission to reproduce the substance of this chapter from *Distorted Images*.]

This baroque structure of myths constructed over the centuries, is the means by which men cling to their masculine pride while sitting at their desks doing a job that a woman could do just as well or better. But if she could, then who the hell are we? To ask men to allow women into this dream castle is to ask them to dismantle it, to admit that nothing is taking place in this office, at this desk but work without glory, without special significance. Man's world is no longer special, but ordinary, no longer a heavy burden with earned privileges, but merely the same world as every other human being's. As women push into man's world, demolishing the ancient prerogatives, they are destroying man as God, reducing him to human proportions.[1]

It is clear from the contributions to this book that women face discrimination in the workplace, and that there are a number of different ways of tackling this. In this chapter, I want to argue that the distorted way in which men and women see one another is at the heart of the problem, and that we have to understand this before we can make headway. I also wish to indicate the ways in which Christian teaching has reinforced the discrimination and prejudice shown against women in the workplace.

Although there are some men or women who do jobs typically done by the other sex, job segregation is still marked. Those women who do traditionally male jobs—for example, in the fire service, or in the building trade for example—are especially likely to meet with opposition, and direct sexual harassment. Harassment may be particularly severe in the workplace setting because men feel this to be their territory, and resist women's intrusion into it—as Korda notes. Men have traditionally proved their masculinity through their jobs. This depends on paid work being perceived as *non-feminine*, since men cannot prove their masculinity by doing tasks of which women are equally capable. The wage packet is the 'particular prize of masculinity in work,' says Willis of manual jobs, 'held to be central, not simply because of its size, but because it is won in a masculine mode in confrontation with the 'real' world which is too tough for the women.[2] This can be problematic for men at a time of high unemployment. The association between middle-class masculinity and employment may be less overt, but is equally real. The women managers interviewed by Cooper and Davidson felt under pressure from the stereotypical attitudes of the men with whom they worked.[3]

Paid work can only affirm masculine identity if women cannot do the same jobs, or cannot do them as well. This can create difficulties, since women clearly do many jobs which are highly skillful, or require valuable qualities, or which are sheer hard physical work. Jobs which women do, and the women who do them, tend to be downgraded. Women spending long hours doing boring work in poor conditions are said not to mind. The implication, sometimes stated, is that women are not capable of minding, being unintelligent and naturally suited to such work. Similar attributes are given to minority ethnic groups. White feelings of superiority are confirmed by the belief that black people cannot do the work. White women may exclude black women from a similar desire to preserve the status of a particular job. Women of colour face double discrimination on the grounds of race and sex, and tend to be the most exploited group of workers in Britain.

Masculinity is linked to paid work not only because doing the task confirms masculinity, but because the main male role in our society is to be the breadwinner. Men are still expected to be able to support their families, and if they cannot perform that role, they can feel truly emasculated. This seems to hold for men in all walks of life although it may be that for some groups beset by chronic and long-term unemployment, masculinity is proved in other ways than through employment. In fact for some groups of women such as those of West Indian origin, it is part of the female role to be a good breadwinner. For some husbands, it is crucial that their wives either do not earn, or earn much less than they do. Their masculinity is threatened by their wives economic independence. This is why some women give up their own jobs when their husbands become unemployed, in an attempt by them to maintain their husband's ego.

The assumption that women do not properly belong in the labour market has led in the past to a great deal of research on why they should want jobs, and the effect of mothers' employment on their children. When women are needed in the labour market, as happened at the beginning of the 1990s, these questions recede into the background. Yet the effect of concentrating on them has been to render women's employment problematic, whilst men's relation to paid work is left unexamined. Women's reasons for doing paid work have tended to be denigrated, though in many respects they parallel those of men. The need to relate to other people becomes the desire for a good gossip. The need to make a contribution to society through creative or useful work becomes a desire to get out of the house. Both sexes gain a sense of identity and worth through paid work and the social relations they have through it. Women value the identity and autonomy it offers them, whilst for men it is associated with masculinity. It is important to note these shared experiences, for they indicate that the world of employment is not a male preserve which women relate to only casually.

Though employment is important for women, because it has not been central to their sexual identity, they are less prone to letting it take over their lives. Women may use a job as an escape from domestic responsibilities, but are less likely to use it as a substitute for relationships. Warning bells are sometimes sounded about the emergence of a new hard breed of female who abandons her femininity and her family for the sake of her career. There are some women who have bought into this system, and it is difficult even for those who want to do things differently. It still seems to be the case that women need to be better than men to succeed, yet they are blamed for being unfeminine if they do. Nonetheless, a lot of women put a great deal of energy into trying to have both a successful job and a fulfilled family life—and that is why so many women feel under pressure. Women are often associated with the gentler virtues of caring and tenderness, and this leaves men free to pursue success in a harsh competitive world. But if women too are seeking only fulfilment, wealth and ambition, society seems doomed. Michael Korda reflects this when he writes: '... the unfamiliar spectacle of a woman ignoring her children to make business trips, focusing her life on success, is an uncomfortable demonstration of just what we, as men, have done in the service of our careers'.[4] The answer is not to discourage women from having careers, so that they may continue to be the carriers of virtue, but to challenge damaging patterns of work and encourage men to change their behaviour. At its most patronising, men could think in terms of setting women a good example!

Yet men are not necessarily happy about opening up traditionally male jobs to women. They can cope with one or two token women, for this may even add to the job's status: we're open to women, but it's far too difficult a job for all but the most exceptional. Men may begin to get uncomfortable, however, when the percentage of women grows. If significant numbers of women enter 'male' jobs, the status drops, and it becomes less attractive to men. It is interesting to speculate whether women's ordination and leadership in the Church will eventually turn it into a female 'ghetto', with no men coming at all. Since an all-male leadership has not brought men in, it may be that female leadership would bring more men in. They would not feel that the only place for men in a church was up-front.

As women enter larger numbers of male jobs, so the remaining male bastions fight hard to retain their exclusivity by overt or subtle means. Many reasons are given as to why women should be excluded from a particular male sphere. In their own context, they may seem reasonable, but it is striking how the same arguments are repeated. The first stage is to say that women cannot do the work, being physically or mentally incapable. John Stuart Mill's point is valid here: 'What women by nature cannot do, it is quite superfluous to forbid them from doing. What they can do, but not so well as the men who are their competitors, competition suffices to exclude them from'.[5]

The second stage is to say that women ought not to do it—because it offends in some way their essential femininity, or God, or both. Opponents of women's ordination often fall into this bracket. The third stage is to agree there are not theoretical problems, but to highlight practical difficulties. The Church of England was in this position in the 1980s over women's ordination. It is an argument commonly cited in employment. For example, firms will say they would like to bring women in, but do not have the toilet facilities.

Finally, the argument will be that women will not fit in. This is unanswerable in some respects. A good working life is based on good relationships between people. Introducing someone unfamiliar with the 'culture' will disturb things—though of course disturbance can have very positive results. Many of the older professions have their roots in exclusively male traditions, and men within in them may fight very hard to preserve what is familiar. Ironically, though the talk may be of preserving standards, totally incompetent men can be

protected within a profession for years, whilst highly able women
are left out. This is immensely frustrating for women who are outside
an organisation fighting to get in. It is seen clearly in the Roman
Catholic Church and in the Church of England, where male priests
can function inadequately for years in parishes or be put in office
based jobs to keep them out of the way, whilst women are denied
the chance even to test their vocation.

There may or may not be a conscious desire to exclude women,
but as Mead says, when women try to enter previously male jobs,
'the whole pattern of thought, the whole symbolic system within
which the novice must work, facilitates every step taken by the
expected sex, obstructs every step taken by the unexpected sex'.[6] It is
sometimes suggested that general manners between men and women
show that women are felt to be visitors: chairs are pulled out for
them, doors held open. No wonder women who feel themselves to be
equals find these shows of respect from men unnerving. they introduce
sex where it should be irrelevant, and indicate that women do not
belong.

Sexual harassment conveys a similar message. It is difficult to
define sexual harassment exactly, because it is not the act but the
way it is experienced which marks it as harassment. Much of the
touching, flirting and joking that goes on between the sexes in the
workplace is not sexual harassment, because it is mutual. Sexual
behaviour becomes harassment when it is unwanted and intrusive,
and is at its most problematic where there is an unequal power
relation between harasser and victim, so that the victim cannot deal
with it. Wise and Stanley say that a composite workplace definition
of sexual harassment suggests it is 'repeated and unreciprocated
actions, comments and looks of sexual nature and which treat the
recipient as a sexual object only. It prejudices the recipient's job
security or promotion prospects and/or creates a stressful working
environment. Generally the recipient is a woman and the harasser is
a man, although it isn't unknown for a man to be harassed'. Yet, they
point out, speaking of it in this way separates it off from other forms
of sexism, and lets people think it can be solved simply, through
legislation or tribunals.[7]

Although sexual harassment is common in the world at large
there may be particular reasons why it occurs in the workplace. For
example, it may represent a misguided attempt to make human contact (as it may outside the workplace too). Hearn and Parkin note
high levels of harassment in industries characterised by alienating

work conditions, and lack of control of the product and act of production. They wonder whether 'harassment could be interpreted as an attempt to create some human contact as part of or in reaction to this alienation, or just another alienated working act'.[8]

As Hearn and Parkin show, sexuality pervades organisations, and not only in the more obvious ways. Some organisations, such as the pornography industry, may have sexual goals. Others use sex in the course of what they do, for example, advertising, or the use of women to facilitate business deals. Military establishments promote a particular kind of aggressive, heterosexual masculinity, with 'woman' and 'queer' being the most frequent insults hurled at each new recruit. The tough image of military manhood helps to attract recruits, and to 'sustain the morale and self-esteem of the men already in uniform'. Women in the forces are a threat, because their presence threatens that masculine image of military life.[9]

Many organisations have unofficial initiation ceremonies that are sexual in tone. These are common in men-only organisations, as well as being part of the culture in women's workplaces.[10]

Sexuality is ever-present in organisations, say Hearn and Parkin, yet it can be difficult to pin down. It makes itself felt through ambiguities, innuendo, gossip, and joking, but is seldom talked about publicly and freely. The language and imagery of a predominantly male workplace, 'girlie' calendars, adverts, sex-stereotyping of secretaries, the sneering and sexual joking and horseplay can all serve to make women uncomfortable whilst affirming men's sense of shared masculinity. The rituals of back-slapping, sexist joking, and the constant reminder of heterosexuality, which characterise men's relationships with one another make it difficult for homosexual men within an organisation.

Such behaviour reinforces the idea that women do not belong. If they join in, they are unfeminine; if they opt out or complain, they isolate themselves. Women may create a similar atmosphere which is uncomfortable for men. But the few men in a female workplace are much more likely to be in senior positions, and less likely to suffer harassment.

Sexual harassment of women is a serious problem in the workplace because the harasser is often in a superior position, and if the victim complains, she is in danger of losing her job. The nature of women's jobs also means they are less likely to be free to move around in order to avoid men who harass them. Sexual harassment is widespread, although it is only in recent years that it has been given public recognition. It is common across all kinds of occupations; one would like to think that clergymen were immune, but many women who work for the Church know better. Sexual harassment may be more obvious to women entering traditionally male jobs, because they expected to be treated as equals. Women in more traditional female jobs often just accept it as normal behaviour from the men with whom they work.

It seems that sexuality in the workplace is at once pervasive, and seen to be irrelevant. The hard-working male manager may see himself as wedded to the job, in which his sexuality has no place. Yet success and career are often seen as indicators of men's masculinity and sexuality. Wealthy men have an aura of sexuality even if they are physically unattractive. This is perhaps another example of a common situation in the workplace, whereby men's weaknesses are interpreted as strengths or ignored, whilst supposed female weaknesses are highlighted and used to exclude them. A similar mechanism occurs when the dominant White group defines Black people as different, and denies them opportunity on that basis. There are a number of versions around of a piece which compares attitudes towards women and men:

He's ambitious	She's pushy
He's having lunch with the boss – he must be doing well	She's having lunch with the boss—they must be having an affair
He gets on well with people at work	She's always gossiping
He's moving on—he must be a good worker	She's moving on—women are so unreliable

and so on[11]

Women are highly visible when they step out of their traditional roles. This means that professional women in token or lone positions face strains and pressures which dominant members of the organisation do not have: increased performance pressure, visibility, being a test case for future women, isolation, lack of female role models, exclusion from male groups, and distortion of women's behaviour by others to fit them into pre-existing sex stereotypes.[12] These factors operate even where women have been welcomed into a male-dominated profession.

The picture painted in this book is stark, and it is very difficult for both sexes to come to terms with men's denigration and oppression of women. It has been easiest for most of us to pretend it doesn't happen. Pornography or sexual violence may intrude on our consciousness from time to time, women get used to dealing with occasional unwelcome attentions from men, and we snipe at each other in our intimate relationships. But we seldom connect these things together. Most of us lack any sense of the system of patriarchy, which makes women and men view each other with suspicion, and leads to men trying to exert power over women. Perhaps we sense, rightly, that to admit the existence of patriarchy will threaten the delicate balance of our lives together. I spend much of my working and leisure hours in the company of men, barely conscious of gender differences between us. But sometimes a comment or the subject of discussion suddenly puts us on opposite sides, and we experience a fall into division and enmity.

The feminist critique threatens to bring this sense of division into our intimate relationships. Women who have established reasonably comfortable patterns for living with men do not want their lives disturbed. So is there any way of being honest about the evils of male domination whilst maintaining good relationships between men and women?

Part of the answer lies in focusing on the common humanity which we share. This means insisting that men are not evil by nature, any more than women are. Men's suspicions and fear of women, as well as their dependence on and admiration for women, parallel women's attitudes towards men. But the crucial difference is that men have power in society. Inaccurate stereotypes can persist because men are able to determine the definitions used. Where male experience is the norm, women's behaviour can be classified as deviant. Men have dominated for so long in the key institutions of society that it seems normal; we believe in their ability to be impartial. Yet it is inevitable that any group in power will tend to perpetuate its own interests, and this has happened both overtly and unconsciously in the decisions men make.

The challenge of feminism is the insistence that women have as much right to act in and influence the world as do men, and must be treated equally in relationships. This has to be taken on board particularly by men, and the process will be painful. It means acknowledging that the sex to which they belong has done wrong in oppressing women, and that even men who support feminism have benefited from this. And it means a commitment to opposing discrimination and negative attitudes towards women in both public and private spheres. Current ideas about masculinity do hurt men, but for men to concentrate merely on expressing their feelings and healing their own pain is to avoid the issue of their power. Yet asking men to relinquish their power will feel like a threat to their very identity, perhaps even their Christian identity.

For whilst Christianity theoretically recognises the will to dominance and aggression as sin, it seldom indicates that this is a sin to which males in our society may be particularly prone. Indeed, Christian thinking about men's role in society has overwhelmingly accepted that men should be in control—of themselves, of women and of the world. Christians may speak of men being under the lordship of Christ, but otherwise, this view closely parallels what most men think masculinity is all about—being self-assured, unafraid, in control and autonomous, not dependent, and showing leadership or dominance. It is important for Christian men to look at the extent to which Christianity has sanctioned this view of masculinity, with little attempt to make a critique of it. This masculine ideal puts a great strain on men, and for all our sakes, we need to challenge men about their need to feel in control, and the way we speak of God lays on men to work hard and lead wisely. Instead we might emphasise the disturbing spontaneity of the Holy Spirit, and the way that God works through weakness and subverts traditional masculine values.

It is possible to face the fact of male oppression of women squarely, and not deny it in the interests of false harmony, because it matters that men are like that. Recognising that men are not created to be tyrants is the first step in working for change. Nonetheless, we must take seriously the present degree of alienation between the sexes; it is not enough simply to assert their equality before God. Centuries of patriarchy are not overcome by good intention, and we must face up to the deep-rooted misogyny at the heart of our culture and our churches. Male domination within the Church has been justified by a whole edifice of theological assumptions about the necessity of the Godhead being spoken about and represented only in male terms. Acceptance of discrimination against women is enshrined both in church legislation and in the hearts of many Christians. It is true that many Christians do accept the principle of the equality of the sexes.

Some also recognise that the demands of justice entail special measures to oppose the oppression of women. But few churches actively try to reform relationships between the sexes or to transform social systems, and our witness in the world is seriously damaged as a consequence.

The gospel we proclaim holds out an invitation to meet a God who is on the side of the disadvantaged and oppressed, and who liberates us from our distorted attitudes to sexuality and to each other. The *Faith in the City* Report side-stepped the question of women in the Church, but it rightly proclaimed:

It is only when the church itself is sensed to be a community in which all alienation caused by age, gender, race and class is decisively overcome, that its mission can begin to be authentic among the millions who feel themselves alienated, not only from the church, but from society as a whole.[13]

References

1   Korda: *Male Chauvinism,* Hodder & Stoughton, London, 1975, paraphrased from p 63.
2   P Willis: *Learning to Labour,* Saxon House, London, 1977, p 150.
3   C Cooper and M Davidson: *High Pressure,* Fontana, London, 1982.
4   Korda, *Male Chauvinism,* p 86.
5   J Mill, quoted in J Richards: *The Sceptical Feminist,* Routledge and Kegan Paul, London, 1980, p 101.
6   Mead: *Male and Female,* Penguin, Harmondsworth, 1971, p 339.
7   S Wise and L Stanley: *Georgie Porgie,* Pandora, London, 1987, pp 39/41 and 61.
8   Hearn and Parkin, *Sex at Work,* Hemel Hempstead, 1987, p 85.
9   L Segal: *Is the Future Female?,* Virago, London, 1987, p 187 ff.
10 See S Westwood, *All Day Every Day,* Pluto, London, 1984, for example. Though rare, it is not unknown for women to harass other women sexually.
11 This version is taken from R Dawson: *And all that is Unseen,* Church House Publishing, London, 1986, p 39.
12 Cooper and Davidson, *High Pressure,* p 58.
13 *Faith in the City,* Church House Publishing, London, 1985, p 60.

7

Women
in the Making

MARY ROSS

Adolescence as the stage between childhood and adulthood has
interested researchers in various fields of study throughout this
century. It has been seen as a modern invention, created by the combination of a reduction in child labour and the corresponding increase
in compulsory schooling and further education. A central feature of
this phase is the development of identity—that sense by which the
young person comes to 'know' who he/she is. Writing in the late 50s/
early 80s—a time of occupational plenty—Erik Erikson asserted that
a successful transition into adulthood depended on the attainment
of 'work identity'. Thirty years later, with youth unemployment
rising throughout the western world, the eyes of researchers have
turned to the impact of this phenomenon on young people. Emotional
headlines scream at us from many of our newspapers, drawing our
attention to the plight of a 'lost' generation—a generation who are no
longer needed by their society.

Working in Glasgow as an educational psychologist, I was interested in how a group of young teenagers, destined to enter the world
of work in the early 80s, would view their futures. To this end I
embarked on a five year voyage of discovery, accompanying 300
teenagers as they journeyed through the transition from school to
the horizons beyond. A criticism levelled at much of the research in
this area prior to the mid 80s was the lack of attention paid to the
importance of work in the life of girls, not to mention the effects of
unemployment on them. Roberts (1984), surveying youth employ-
ment/ unemployment research, highlights this problem:

> Many pre- and post-war studies of school leavers concentrated
> on boys. Girls unemployment, lack of training and further edu-
> cation were considered less of a problem.

The aim of this chapter is to redress the balance and ensure that the views of the girls participating in the study are represented.

The Research Project

The teenagers were drawn from the third years of two mainstream secondary schools in Glasgow—one non-denominational, the other, Roman Catholic. Both schools draw on the same geographic area and represent a wide variety of parental employment experience. The sample consisted of 140 girls and 180 boys—all 300 having agreed to participate in the study and having their parents' permission to do so. After the initial year of the project all signed a contract to continue to participate in their fourth year and in subsequent follow-up interviews three years later. At the time of writing these post-18 interviews are underway. For the purpose of this chapter I shall confine my comments to the themes emerging from the hopes and fears the teenagers expressed at the onset of the study, when they were 14 years of age.

In order to tap into this rich seam I had asked them to write an essay entitled 'My future'. No guidelines for completion of this initial task were given to avoid the possibility of researcher bias influencing the topics covered.

Themes emerging

In conducting this survey, Roberts (1984) concluded: 'Young people are as able and willing to work as ever, but their jobs have gone'. Although at least two years away from the labour market, all but 8 of these 300 teenagers concentrated their main sights on jobs and careers. Many were already concerned about the decrease in available work and the possibility that they may have difficulty in obtaining a job.

> In the 90s, I hope to be working. I would like to have a good and interesting job and something that I could enjoy as well as work hard in .... I would not spend time studying at University and getting no pleasure out of it. I'd rather find a job and be happy. If I could not find a job I would stay on at school until I am 17 and have more qualifications so that I'd get a good job.   (ALISON)

When I leave school I plan to look for a job, but if I am unsuccessful, I suppose I will go on a YTS as it might help me to get a job. After the YTS and if I don't get kept on, then I will go abroad and get a job there. (LORNA)

These attitudes of the girls were reflected also by the boys:

By the time it is the 90s I would like to have a job—one that I like and that pays well .... If I have to go on a YTS I will. I would not like to be unemployed.

Although only 14 years of age, these teenagers were already focussing their attention on the jobs/careers which they hoped would lie ahead. In fact the girls (90% of them compared to 75% of the boys) led the field in having quite definite occupational goals in mind. No doubt the recent choice of third year subjects may have concentrated their minds a little here.

The girls and boys were very clearly following quite different gender-stereotypical pathways. The girls choices lay mainly in the following areas—teaching (nursery, primary, secondary ... in descending frequencies); nursing (mainly directed towards children's services) and other medical careers, such as radiography, opthamology, physiotherapy; secretarial work; provision of services through employment as shop assistants, travel agents, hairdressers, caterers, chefs, air hostesses, bank clerks. A few were interested in the professions of law and accountancy and there was one mention each of work as a mechanic and an engineer. This list is in marked contrast to the one emerging from the boys' essays. Here their aspirations lie in the directions of engineering (civil, electrical, electronic); motor mechanics; printing; plumbing; brick-laying; welding; electrical and joinery work; glazing; professional sports careers such as footballer, golfer, cyclist and basketball; accountancy, architecture; veterinary medicine and scientific research also featured in this list. Both boys and girls wrote of joining the services, but here again the careers they were hoping to take up were different—with the girls concentrating on office work and nursing while the boys looked to jobs as engineers, soldiers and pilots. This divergence within a service was also apparent when both genders indicated an interest in joining the police force with the boys choosing more active roles. There is an obvious diversion of labour here which may send a shiver down the spine of the General Teaching Council for Scotland ... in the summary leaflet describing their recent policy paper 'Gender in Education', the general principle is enunciated:

> Careers guidance systems should encourage pupils to consider the possibilities of work across traditional sex boundaries. All occupations, even such predominantly single-sex jobs such as nursery-nurse and airline pilot, should be regarded as gender neutral.

In trying to understand the importance of work for today's younger generation, it is necessary to delve more deeply into these teenagers' essays. We can then examine some of the connections they are making between their career choices and other post school trajectories such as marriage and family life.

Money is seen by most of these young people as the currency which enables them to head towards adulthood. However the way in which an earned income forms a linkage between their careers and any subsequent commitments to a marriage partner and children is quite different depending on whether this commodity of money is being viewed through male or female eyes. The boys on the whole fall back on a 'breadwinner' role, describing the necessity for a 'good' wage/salary before they can undertake the responsibilities involved in marriage and family life.

> If I got the job I wanted I would work very hard at it. If I got a good salary I would think about buying myself a house. If this worked out I would then start thinking abut getting married. Then I would settle down with my wife, still working away at my job.
> (STEPHEN)

> When I am older I'll get married, get a house, have kids and have enough money to support them by working.   (JIM)

The girls' approach is quite different—a major theme emerging here being their reliance on a salary as a means to independence and security. A career will provide these sought after goals. Where the girls have addressed this issue, their essays vibrate with determination.

> It will probably take until I am 24 to become fully qualified as an accountant. I don't really want to get married or have children because I don't want to spend my life running after a man and children. If I did get married I would be qualified as an account

already and I would not give up my career for a man. (LINDA)

When I'm a lawyer I will get married .... I would like to open my own law business and be well known .... After a few years I would have a family and then go back to law.   (GAYE)

Not for them the fall back on a domestic role in life!

After I have a good and steady job I would like to get married at about 25 and later have a family. I will stay at work until I retire and not become a housewife.   (LYNSEY)

Some draw on their mothers' experience to support their points of view:

I would like to get a degree and I hope for a job. At this time I would still be living at home until I am married. I would not have any children until my late 20s or early 30s as I would like a career. My mum has regretted giving up everything and having given up an early career. I don't want to make the same mistake as her! You learn from other people's mistakes!

(SANDRA)

Whatever the chosen career of the girls who indicated that they hoped to marry in the future and/or have children only one saw her life as revolving round the domestic scene:

I wish to marry but finish my College or University courses first. After then I will hopefully meet someone and marry and then hopefully my life will revolve round having a family. If this does happen, it will be a dream come true although I don't think this will all come about as easily as I have written.

This interconnection between work and marriage is of vital importance, especially at a time when the figures for marriages in difficulties and youth unemployment are rising at an alarming rate. Both male and female participants in this present study point to the inter-connectedness of work and love commitment. Sigmund Freud made the connection when asked to define a 'sane' person ... this he did in terms of one who could both love and work. Clearly the young teenagers here are beginning to look ahead to '... how they can best find personal satisfaction in the adult world of love and work' (Kroger, 1989).

Not all those teenagers who mentioned marriage in their essays did so in a positive way. Another thread running through the work of a few was their determination not to marry. Of those who mentioned marriage, one boy had no intentions of future wedded bliss:

> I would not like to get married, because I would feel I would get tied down: and need to do things and not just what I wanted to do.
> (HUGH)

This fear of being tied down is one of the main reasons given by the ten girls who echoed Hugh's concern:

> I think when I leave school, jobs will be hard to get. So I want to do as well in school as I can. I do not want to get married because I want to be able to have a career and to travel about and do as I please. I want to be successful.   (DEIRDRE)

The wish not to be tied down is primarily behind the emphasis the girls place on delaying marriage until they reach their mid 20s. For many of them marriage is already viewed as a brake on their freedom.

There are some interesting points of contact in the essays of both genders. For example, all those who mention having children almost all opt for the statutory two! In addition their sights are set on one of each variety! However it is only the girls who have gone so far as to name them.

> I don't want to get married straight away but when I do get married, if I do, I would like to have 2 children—one girl called Natalie Jane and one boy called Damien—because I like those names.   (DEBBIE)

> I would like to get married but not until I was at least 22. I would like 2 children—one boy and one girl. I would call the boy David and the girl Sarah-Jane.   (ANGELA)

Other common patterns in the essays of girls and boys include their sights being set on the acquisition of a driving licence, a car and a flat. Also many of them indicate that they intend living and working abroad. In the latter case the boys normally give as their rationale the state that Britain, Glasgow or their local area is in, whereas the girls more often than not reflect positive reasons for their choice: for example, a love of travel.

Returning to the topic of careers, a difference emerges in how the boys and the girls envisage their entry into the labour market. As in days of yore, the boys often place reliance on family contacts to help them gain access to their chosen job:

> I want to get a job in The .... as a printer and just now my father works there and he has put my name down as a van boy. My name will come up for a job in about 2 years.
>
> (ANTHONY)

> I would hope to have the qualifications to go to University and study law. After that I would get experience from working in my uncle's office and then with financial support from my family I would hope to start up my own lawyer's practice.   (BRIAN)

There are many examples of this dependence on family 'know-how' on the boys part, but hardly any such references for the girls. The following is one of the few:

> When I leave school I want to be a hairdresser. My big sister knows a hairdressers and the people who work in it and they said I can work in there, washing hair and brushing the floor.
>
> (SUSAN)

There is general agreement that qualifications are helpful and in some cases necessary, but this male reliance on 'who you know' harks back to the halcyon days of apprenticeships. On the other hand, it is in the girls essays that we see a very different connection between career choice and their family experience. As mentioned earlier, many of the girls' jobs target young children and in most cases the girls state that they 'like' or 'love' this age group. This turns out to be based on experience since most of them refer to their involvement in quite an amount of child minding ... perhaps the days of child labour are not over! There is only one boy who claims to 'like children a lot' and gives this as his reason for wanting to have a family of his own.

Apart from the usefulness of having a parent in the place of employment they want to enter, little reference is made to following in their parents' footsteps. A couple of examples are given below:

> I would like to work in a travel agents. I have an idea what it
> would be like and what it involves as my mum works in one.
>
> (JULIE)

One teenager is not so sure . . .

> In my future I will expect to get a decent job as an office worker
> or follow in my dad's footsteps to be an electrician, but I would
> like to play for Rangers.   (IAN)

Another feature of the boys projections is their concerns with
possible future drug abuse, crime and subsequent prison sentences:

> If I didn't get all that I hoped to get I don't want to end up being
> a drunk or taking drugs or anything like that.   (GERRY)

> I just want to grow up and get on with life, not taking drugs or end-
> ing up in prison.   (ROBERT)

These concerns are not expressed by any of the girls. The only potential disaster mentioned by one girl was an unwanted pregnancy, but in
her own words, 'I'm not that daft!'

The enterprise culture of the Thatcherite era has certainly influenced many of these young teenagers. Across a wide spectrum of
jobs, many are already looking to the day when they will have their
own business. The boys are a bit more venturesome here, but this is
more a reflection of the difficulty the girls would have in trying to
branch out into the private business arena, given the nature of the
jobs they have chosen. It is not so easy for a relatively young adult to
set up their own business if they are recently trained in teaching,
nursing *etc*; whereas the boys who have opted for trades would find
it possible to branch out on their own.

Final Reflections

As can be seen from the above, there are often differences between the
two genders in their career aspirations and their hoped-for mode of
entry to them; differences in how they view marriage and family

life—money often has a different value for boys and girls at this stage of their development. Among the various areas of agreement, by far the most important is the overwhelming desire to be a full member of the 'working class'. Of particular concern is the apparent lack of awareness they exhibit of a major change in the adult world of work, namely that changes of occupation are now commonplace in adulthood; they are no longer the exception. In no way are these young teenagers signalling their readiness for a flexible career structure. They are not at a stage where they can contemplate 'work' abstractly and experience themselves as a working person. They thus fall back on Erikson's model using a specific career choice to act as their bearer across the difficult waters flowing between childhood and the adult world that awaits them. As mentioned earlier this model was born at a time when young people could choose a career from a range appropriate to their ability level. Reliance on it now can only increase the gap between their hopes (or worse, their expectations) and the possibilities. This is particularly important in considering the girls' futures. If these 140 girls are representative of many others, then their strong desire for a career identity when viewed against the harsh reality of the current unemployment figures and their unwillingness to enter the domestic arena as an alternative, must surely put many girls at risk. In spite of Government claims to the contrary, there are not enough appropriate training places to go round. With the removal of the 16-18 year olds from the unemployment register, this could throw many girls into early marriages and/or parenting roles. These situations are well known to be particularly vulnerable as the partners rarely have a 'good-enough' grasp of their *own* identities, let alone of one anothers. This makes for quite a paradox ... when the young themselves are recognising that they are not ready for marriage and family commitments, and are indicating that they wish to delay undertaking them until their mid-20s, the very activity which would help in this delay—employment—is less available to them.

There is another aspect worth considering here. These teenagers already have a pretty good grasp of the inter-connectedness which Freud referred to simply as 'Lieben und arbeiten'—love and work —enable a person to be and to remain sane. Once again I turn to Roberts to focus our attention on a possible consequence of this intimate relationship for this generation:

> Maintaining or repairing the bridges that supported traditional transitions will not prepare today's youth for their futures. They

must learn flexibility and adaptability, to disengage as well as to attach themselves to occupations, sexual and domestic companions.

The majority of the teenagers speaking out of these pages are looking to a future which contains one career and one marriage partner. The fluctuations in the employment market may bring with it a corresponding changeability in choice of partners. If this is what lies ahead for this rising generation, they are going to require a great deal of support as such a scenario is not one they are presently prepared for. Social organisations, themselves trying to cope with their own changing identities will need to muster all their resources to stand by young people as they enter the next millennium. By then this particular group will be over 25 years of age—out of the 'youth' and 'young people' categories. They, in fact, will be the parents of the next generation. I give the last word to one of the girls:

All in all my life in the 90s won't be too eventful, but 2000 onwards will be!   (NICOLA)

References

General Teaching Council: *Gender in Education*, Leaflet No 8, May 1992.

J Kroger: *Identity in Adolescence—The Balance between Self and Other*, Routledge, 1989.

K Roberts: *School Leavers and their Prospects—Youth and the Labour Market in the 1980s*, Open University Press, 1984.

8

Martha and Mary at the Pearly Gates: a Theological Fantasy

ELIZABETH TEMPLETON

The presupposition of this dialogue is the playful suggestion than in the twinkling of an eye which brings Martha and Mary to the life of the resurrection allows them a bird's eye view of the rest of human history en route!

Martha: You appreciate of course that I'm going to be the one who gets the kudos in here. I've been the one who's kept our existence afloat for the last twenty years, day in day out, while you swan about doing anything you fancy.

Mary: I doubt it, After all, that time when Jesus stayed with us he seemed to think that I'd chosen the better part. An enlightened guy for his times, recognising that the drudgery of sweeping floors and washing pots wasn't what a woman's life was all about.

Martha: Rubbish! A typical male who thought it quite appropriate that everything should be dropped when he was around, and had no sense at all of the constraints which are involved if you want a meal on the table at a set time. Well I wasn't going to massage his ego. If he was all that keen we should both be able to listen, he could have helped with getting the vegetables ready.

Mary: Come off it! I know we've just zipped through the rest of world history on the way here, and seen how feminism's come a long way, but you can't actually have any real sense of history if you think a Jewish man of his day could have sat down with women and washed cucumbers.

Martha: Well, why not? If he was radical enough to talk to strange women at wells, what was to stop him? And if he was God incognito, as you seem to think, shouldn't he have been able to look at things from the vantage-point of the future? Couldn't he have got this justice for all thing off the ground a bit more effectively? Couldn't he have left his followers one or two more radical parables about the emancipation of women? Or a few explicit prophecies that the keys of his kingdom were for little children to wield, or blacks, or the handicapped?

Mary: But that's what he was saying. Only they all missed the point, the ones who carried on the message. Or they got bits of it, but not the full implications. All his stuff about The first shall be last: or Woe unto you if you put a millstone round the neck of these little children—all that was full of subversive, revolutionary potential, once you actually took time to analyse who actually are the first and the last. But you have to stop doing the dishes for long enough to work that out!

Martha: Thanks a million, sister. You think you're the superior, paid-up feminist consciousness of the New Testament, do you? Got the inner secrets, while poor silly Martha overheard snippets from the kitchen? Well I tell you, when we get to the head of this damned queue, I'm going to have a few words with Mr God and son. First he lets the most potent myth in the book be about a Fall from grace and pleasant pottering in the garden, where food grows off trees, and clothes aren't needed—to a state of existence where war is inevitable for men and childrearing and associated chores left to the women. Then after centuries of that myth calling the tune, Son has the witlessness to say to a married man that he has the power of the keys of the kingdom; and that sets up another few millennia of women's work being defined as stitching altar-cloths, and having lunch ready when the men come back from synod, and looking after the kids while the world gets messed around by generals and lawyers and politicians who wouldn't know baking-soda from cocaine.

Mary: Aren't you being a bit strident, Martha? I mean, neither of us fits the standard pattern of childrearing women, but neither of us fits the pattern of frustrated spinster either. Or of women who were dictated to by husbands. We had great freedom there at Bethany. You loved making the place nice. You loved seeing it straight and sweet and tended. You enjoyed going out for rushes for the floor. You used to say how creative you felt it was to be bringing order out of chaos, like God in creation! You liked to see the copper gleaming and the room full of flowers. You were content, even fulfilled by it. Is all this sourness because it didn't suit me as well? Do we all have to be like each other? That seemed to me to be your chosen work!

Martha: Yes it was. I did like it. I felt that it was my form of creativity. I wasn't pining for anything else, It gave me my identity, just looking round the room, and seeing flowers and polished wood, and trimmed lamps, and linen that smelled of sun-baked herbs, and seeing people relax round a meal, and enjoy new bread, and a stew that was eaten in half an hour, but had taken three to make. And knowing that people liked to come here out of the hubbub, and enjoy the kind of space and tranquillity that only comes from someone in the background who does all that quiet, repetitive, obvious stuff with care. And then I zoom through history with you on the way to this endplace, which is supposed to put every-thing into perspective, and I feel cheated. Because all the current politically correct thinking seems to be saying that I'm an abused and unconscientised throwback. Work has to be paid work, work in the public arena, work on equal terms with men.

Women like me are exploited, physically and emotionally, unless we're shrieking and wailing about under-achievement. But you seem to me to be undermining what was my good life. And as we passed the centuries, I found that was a recurrent delight for many of us; farmers' wives in rural Scotland, suburban house-wives in Barcelona, grandmothers in Syria, even unmarried girls here, there and everywhere. And you feminists march in and say that we're letting the side down, that paid employment is a right —(but you mean a duty, because if we don't all do it or want it, it weakens your case!)—that women who want the primary home-maker role, with or without children, are prisoners of the system, needing liberation, underdeveloped, victims of male demands and expectations.

But that seems as oppressive to me as any patriarchal account. It doesn't let me say, 'This is my work and I enjoy it'. And I think it's wonderful for work not to be connected with pay, or set hours or a structure of pension rights. I love being able to stop when I want, or to meet a neighbour in the market and talk for an hour, or to sit in the garden in the afternoon and sew things, knowing that if I fall asleep in the sun, I'm not in breach of any contract. That's freedom, and I don't feel you recognise it. So, if there's any justice in this place, I only hope I get a chance to speak on my own!

Mary: Well, I'm afraid that just proves that you've gone through the whole journey in space/time with your eyes shut. Or with them open, but so blinkered that you effectively don't see. Didn't you notice all that waste of talent? Women who spent their days sewing samplers or firescreens, but had the capacity to be diplomats or translators or carpenters, and couldn't possibly be because of the social patterns? Men who could have entered the imaginative world of their children much better than their mothers, but couldn't do it because that would have defined them as wimps? Didn't you see these old Greek women bent under loads of firewood while their men sat in cafés drinking? Didn't you see the children of Europe's urban poor, where girls had so much less chance than their brothers of going on at school, because it was assumed that they'd get married, and could be early wage-earners until that point. That's what I'm going to stand for when I see God. The defence of the non-obvious people who can't speak for themselves. That's what I think Jesus was on about. And your zoom through history seems to me not to have taught you that to see people who are not obvious, to notice, to have fresh visions of things, you sometimes have to stop washing the dishes; it's a sign that we're talking about a completely different order of valuing things—a celebration of the weak, as they are, not an attempt to make them justified by the values of the strong. That's why I was commended for stopping work. In that world we've just come from, you have to be able to prove yourself. I think the Jesus-revolution was about saying 'Stuff that'. Your value is not measurable. You are simply valued. You are not worth what you produce, whether it's boots or cars or flower arrangements or clean beds or children: you are valued because you are irreplaceable, and capable of love.

Martha: But that's your idealistic nonsense coming out again. You stand in this queue, wanting admission to the kingdom of heaven because you think you're on the side of the angels. You even have the temerity to say I'm not. But you have no realism whatever about work, or about women's role in it. You fly flags for the breaking down of stereotypes, this radical woman who wouldn't be bullied into the kitchen, but you haven't the remotest sense of how the world works.

If dishes are to be washed three times a day at least, and people to have clean clothes, and the home to be a place where you can sit without being washed and ironed around, and you're not in the superclass which can buy off its obligations with nannies and cooks and private schools, then you're going to need people to do all that; and for the most part they're going to be women, because they are the ones who first bond with their children, and while they're feeding them they generally want to be near them, and that means being home-based.

And being home-based they acquire the skills that men might just as well acquire but don't usually; noticing when a floor needs wiped, doing dishes while talking to the children, thinking what has to be bought for the next three days eating, checking whether there are clean clothes. And once they've acquired them it's so much easier to go on doing it than to put up with the clumsy fuss men make about doing the same thing, that most of us go on doing it after the children are big enough and have left home. And that gives us space. Space to make days flexible, to give and receive hospitality with friends, to have hours free for other people's emergencies, to be able to drop everything in a crisis without consulting the boss .... Now don't you tell me that's all captivity, because I know it's a kind of freedom, and all these emancipated women we met in the last few centuries don't have it. They were as screwed up as the men, chasing deadlines and unavailable, pushing kids and husbands away so that they could get on with their work. You may think that's freedom, but I don't, so if this place is about recognising freedom when you see it, I'll be in.

Mary: But my dear Martha, that's all very well for you. You liked it, and had a gift for it. (Though I do ask myself the question whether you would have liked it if you hadn't been conditioned to think it was your proper place in life as housekeeper for our old parents as they grew unable to manage.) But look at the millions and millions who've hated it, and found no way out. Look at the big scale picture, a kind of black economy made up of hours and hours of unpaid work, and not just unpaid in monetary terms, but so taken for granted that men and children complained bitterly when it didn't happen: 'Mum, you've not done my blouse.' 'Where's my other blue sock?' 'Haven't we got any mustard?' Think of all those women who would have liked to paint, or to go on with their education, or to do something like running a travel agency, and couldn't even try it. Who were cowed by the slogan 'A woman's place is in the home', so that even if they did move into some other sphere of creative life, they felt responsible for everything at home too.

Martha: But don't you think God meant us not all to be doing the same thing? I mean, don't you think its more natural for women to be home-based, nurturing, humanising, and less so for men? Isn't that tied up with biology and body chemistry, and centuries of evolution? Isn't it flying in the face of a proper respect for creation to be denying all that? The societies which don't go fussing and fretting about roles, but simply live in the comfortable patterns of the ages seemed to me much happier as we came through them on the way here. No self-consciousness, no self-examination, just a mutual recognition that you fitted into a way of life which worked.

Mary: I don't think you've understood anything. It wasn't God who made men to go out and be hunter-gatherers and women to be home-based mothers. *We* did that. Obviously when we were barely distinguishable from the animals, we were tied to instinctive patterns that belonged to the past. But being human, being Adam/Eve is about belonging to the future, and having the responsibility to show that to the rest of creation. It means not being defined by the strictures of biology. Look at that amazing catalogue of freedoms human beings have made for themselves, words and music and paint that let them out of the cage of the present; technology that lets them conquer space and be relieved of most of their physical labour. Don't you see, we're moving beyond the role definitions of male and female in the same way? Anyone can do anything. If you can't face that, or want it, or enjoy it, you're not going to have much pleasure in the freedom of this place. Even for earth, you're earthbound.

Martha: You're so smug! Of course some things change because you've got technology! You can stop women washing dishes by inventing dishwashers, and you can change social patterns so that men and women both go out to work, and you have a new under-class of other people (usually women!) who are paid to look after the children you don't want to look after unpaid (though you brought them into the world). But you don't tell me that any amount of technology wipes a child's tears the way its mother does, nor any substitute with diplomas in child care! All the bonding of those first weeks and months doesn't just evaporate with weaning you know! Or are you going to tell me that breast-feeding is an undesirable throwback to our biological past as well, and that freedom means bottle-feedbanks with tape-recorded human voices to create the illusion of company!

Mary: Come on! Don't get hysterical! I'm sure that women have a special marvellous intimacy with their children which nothing else replaces. But that's been made the pretext for a great deal of other stuff which has nothing to do with human well-being at all. There's no reason why fathers can't wipe eyes as tenderly as mothers. And there's no essential connection between child care and housework, just an accidental one which has suited men for centuries. What we're all made for is to realise our fullest poten-tial, and that means sharing the negative bits of experience and work as widely and fairly as possible, and giving as many people as possible the chance of fulfilment. And, systematically, the difficulty for women of having the right to work has been enforced by the world's social patterns. So its a major breakthrough to have got recognition that you either have the right to work where you like outside the home, or the right to be paid for a day's work if you stay in it.

Martha: But what's so great about work? You're saying it's much more important than I am, in a funny kind of way. I think most of it is only done because it has to be, to keep the world ticking, to make money, to keep the economy going! There's nothing to celebrate about work as such, is there? You don't think the king-dom of God's about work conditions do you?

Mary: Well, I hope its not about a great eternal sauna bath of infinite leisure anyway. Work is part of our dignity, our identity. You know how demoralised people get when they don't have work. It's an expression of what our skills and gifts are. It's a contribution to the fabric of society. It's ....

Martha: Aren't you taking over my lines?!

Mary: Not at all. I've never been against work. I've just been against having the kind of work defined for me in advance! And being so stuck in it that you haven't the ability to stop, to take control of your own life, to have space. For me, Jesus and his kingdom authorise me to want that, to claim it, to enjoy it. You're the one who lets work be the be all and end all.

Martha: I think you're starry-eyed. I'm the realist. I recognise that most work for most people has to be got on with. But it's not creative or expressive of their identity for most people, men or women. It's often routine, boring, unpleasant or even dangerous. but its part of the human lot, for better or worse, and we have to get on with it. Sure, for some people with the luxury of choice, its a pleasure to do what they do, at least on the whole, and even more of a pleasure to get paid for it. But for the vast majority of all the people we saw in the history that flashed past us on the way here, work was only just bearable because it fed and clothed them. It seems to me that if you've any solidarity with the vast majority of people and their longings, you'd know that they'd love to be shot of work, and get on with all the things they'd really much rather be doing, gardening, or making love, or reading a book, or tinkering with their cars, or birdwatching.

Mary: Now you're stealing my lines! That's what I mean by creative space! but with all the possibilities that history's thrown up, work didn't need to be boring and dreary. That sort of thing is a matter of social planning, and if women had had more say in it all, in how offices are run, and businesses and factories, I bet they'd be more humane and pleasant places than they are now, and more fulfilling.

Martha: I do think you're overdoing this fulfilment stuff! And anyway what's all that got to do with the values of our precious Jesus. Not much self-fulfilment about him. Turn the other cheek and end up on a cross! All that seems a bit at odds with revolutionary feminism, doesn't it? I'd have thought all the force of your convictions would have had you saying the opposite. When you're abused, put up with it, for Jesus' sake? Isn't that more like all these suffering servants and martyrs that the traditions are full of? Isn't that the virtue of patience and longsuffering and so on?

Mary: Not at all! That's about the personal choices you make. You can't even begin to make personal choices if you're so defined by your social position that you've no freedom at all.

Martha: No one's ever like that. The slave in Uncle Tom's Cabin couldn't be robbed of his integrity and freedom even when he was absolutely constrained in his physical limitations. Stone walls do not a prison make, nor kitchen sinks. It's all a matter of how you deal with them, what attitude you take, whether you can rise above the situation.

Mary: But Martha, that's too heroic, too abstract for most people. The God of Jesus didn't tell people to rise above things. He brought them out of bondage, he encouraged them to get up and leave Egypt. He healed the sick, he didn't tell them to rise above it. All the history of salvation is about transforming things that are damaging us and creation. We're enlisted in that battle. You can't be so fatalistic and say, 'That's the way things are always going to be, but just be a stoic and it won't get to you. The reason Jesus finished up on a cross was because he tackled it all, tackled the oppressors, tackled the Pharisees, tackled the powers that be. Listening to him taught me that, and that's what made it right for women to challenge the specific oppressions that they'd received at the hands of a world largely defined up till then by men.

Martha: But don't you see what a great con trick that is. Paid work is itself a kind of oppression for most people. To be at someone else's beck and call! To have to be here at a certain time! To have to be assessed and adjudicated depending on one's performances! Even to have to earn money! None of that, I'm sure will be happening in the kingdom of God. So is it not just judging as the world does to put so much emphasis on it as a right, far less a privilege. Wouldn't it be more in line with your Jesus's sermon on the mount to say, 'Live like a lily of the field. Be decorative. Enjoy the weather. Add to the environment of those around you. Forget about being busy, busy, busy. Learn from the birds of the air'.

Mary: But you're not a bird. You're a human being. And it's our responsibility to do all these things that human beings do. We were given a world to live in that needs builders and farmers and economists and hairdressers and vets, because we couldn't survive without them.

Martha: Without hairdressers!

Mary: Well, in a sense. If you're not going to go all puritan about it, work includes all these thinks that make for people's wellbeing— entertainment, decoration, music, as well as food and drink and shelter. (That's another reason why Jesus commended me for taking time to sit and listen for its own sake, without trying to combine it with doing the mending or preparing vegetables.) Work is all these things, the activities that make life worth living, rich and full and diverse and complex, and you can't get out of it without being in some funny way detached from you common humaness. Whether or not you're paid for this or that work, and how much it's worth are, I agree, two different questions, but you can't be workless and human!

Martha: Rubbish! Think of children, of old people, of the unem- ployed, of New Age travellers. I'm the one who's had the repu- tation for centuries of being the workaholic, but you're actually idealising work more than I ever have. And you claim to be tying that up with big themes like emancipation for women! I'm sug- gesting that there's another freedom which lets women challenge the Protestant work ethic, and affirm the importance of just being- there, being-there-for-others, as that man Tillich put it about Jesus. I want to challenge all this 'What do you do?' way into people's identity, and to be able to listen, instead to the 'Who are you?' questions. You should be able to appreciate that, of all people.

Mary: But who you are *is* what you do! That's the core of people's sense of value.

Martha: Well, it shouldn't be. Isn't that what you got into all the books for? Our value comes from loving and being loved. That's what kept the hostages going in a Lebanese cell when they were absolutely impotent. It's what makes people able to handle the huge terrors of age and infirmity and retirement. It's what makes small children happy with themselves. Of course people often are valued for what they do, for their usefulness. But that's secondary. If it becomes primary, even to them, and certainly to others, they are being valued as instruments to something else.

Mary: Look, this is a ridiculous argument. You keep talking about high and mighty abstracts. I'm just talking about the concrete state of affairs which is the setting for most human decisions, in politics, in families, in the interactions of human beings. It seems to me that from the beginning, men and women have been meant to share the responsibility for all that.

Martha: But with women very much defined as secondary, helpers, auxiliaries. Not as equals. The ideals of equality, of rights, of opportunity, of education and so on are late ideas of the European secular Enlightenment. They've got nothing to do with God of the Old and New Testaments. The church was just scrabbling to keep abreast of the trends in the world around it, and feminism happened to be one of them in the late twentieth century. I think that's extremely difficult to reconcile with what is the much deeper strain of Biblical understanding, that women are subordinate to men in the order of creation, and fulfil their vocation primarily in supporting and maintaining the life of the family. I mean, it can't just be coincidence that it's precisely in cultures like the United States and Western Europe, where the strongest battles for women's right to work were fought, that the family has disintegrated fastest, with soaring divorce rates and major problems in inter-generational life.

Mary: Granted, but that may prove just what an instrument of oppression families could be, so that the struggle for justice within it, like the struggle against apartheid, needed a very basic dismantling of the old structures. That's what all the talk about new wine in old wineskins was about, or the Pauline affirmations about there being neither Jew nor Greek, male nor female in Christ. Whatever the misdeeds of history, that stands for me as a mandate for change. And the right of women to be self-determining, to be economically potent rather than dependent, to have the freedom to move away from stereotyped roles is all part of that.

Martha: But you're the one who's stereotyping! You're not hearing me say that for me it's an insult to be told I was following an obsolete role-model, or colluding with social injustice. I was perfectly happy!

Mary: So what are you going to do now? We're nearly at the end of the queue.

Martha: I'm going to complain about the bad press I've had for so much of history, and appeal for a re-appraisal of my freedom and integrity! and I hope you're knocked off your pedestal a bit as the archetypal liberated woman. Then I hope to do a bit of real living!

Mary: And working?

Martha: Not so you'd recognise it. I've worked enough for a lifetime.

Mary: Then I think you may be in for a shock.

Martha: Maybe we're both in for a shock. What else would heaven be for?

Part III

Stories of
Success and Failure

9

Women—Winners or Losers in the New Europe

CHRISTA SPRINGE

Visions for a New Europe

Everywhere in our world the powerful and strong try to take the law of action into their own hands. This is the case in the building process of a 'New Europe' as well. We want to interfere! We have a vision of participation. And we envisage a just sharing, both of power in decision making and of economic and cultural resources. We do not want any people—be they women or men—to be overlooked and neglected. We do not want Europe to be a big market where human beings and nature are valued only according to their economic usefulness.

The political vision of a Common European House in which people and nationalities live together in peace and with equal rights is for us Christians a familiar and hopeful picture. We, too, use the image of a house—the House of God—in which there are many dwellings and in which the children of God live together. We want to draw up such a brotherly and sisterly way of running a European household.

We want to make our contributions for giving it a shape. Therefore we have to ask the question: who are the architects actually building the New Europe, and who decides to whom each room is to be allocated? Some time ago a West German journalist asked whether women would be sub-tenants of the men or whether they would be able to occupy the house on equal terms and with equal rights? Or will they be assigned the dark economic area in the back yard?

The appealing picture of a common house, used first by Gorbachev, illustrates the problem very vividly. In every traditionally-built house there are preferred situations and rooms, and there are the damp and unlit cellars and backrooms, which are assigned to the servants, the poor relations and to strangers and foreigners. And so will it be with us, too, unless we abandon these draft plans and use all our imagination for feasible alternatives. Or is it already to late? Will women in countries now applying for EC membership have a better chance? Let us discuss this.

Principles and Dangers
of the European Internal Market

Europe is being built as a market place by the strong for the strong. The pattern is not being developed according to the vision of a 'Home' for people, but the 'rules of the house' are being dictated by the principles of the free market economy. The concept of the Internal Market of the European Community has become the guideline for decision making. It becomes clear how little will change for women and for the economically poorer countries when the portions are shared out, and if we keep quiet.

Please allow me to describe briefly the frame work which the European Community (EC) is setting for all the European countries, be they members or not. I am convinced that this frame work deeply effects the situation of women. Only when we know it well we are able to decide what to support, and what to reject.

(i) The European Internal Market

The European Internal Market is an economic power-bloc, built on the principal of a strengthened position in competition with other economic powers and power-blocs (North America and Japan). It is thus a question of superseding and being victorious over others, not of living together'. The aim is to conquer the markets and to defend oneself by outdoing other economic rivals.

– The European of the EC is therefore founded on its own strength at the cost of those who are weaker—in Europe or on other continents.
– Its goals are: economic growth and rising profits. The human aspects are considered to be of less importance.
– A human being is considered as labour on the market, *ie* s/he must have a market value or else s/he is worth nothing.

(ii) The 4 Freedoms

The 4 freedoms which the Internal Market will put into effect are the instruments for the realisation of this principal. They are: freedom of movement for goods, capital, labour-force and services.

Mobility as an opportunity for the labour force—for women as well? Surely for some well qualified and independent women. But not for the majority. For this is not principally about the aim of giving greater opportunities to the individual person, but about disposibility (Verfugbarkeit) within the European labour-market, where they can just be used or be superfluous. If you don't have a job, then you don't profit from it.

Women who have to follow their husbands to another country are mostly losers. They lose their social ties and at the same time their support group. Among other things they lose their own jobs and they have to cope with the double burden of giving stability to their husbands and children in their strange new environment.

I have read about a research carried out at Hannover University amongst students. They were asked whether they were prepared to give up their own job for the partner's sake when s/he would find an attractive new job in another city. Eleven per cent of the women, and 6% of the men agreed to do so. Twenty-five per cent of the married women and 11% of the married men gave a positive reply. That is, in theory, more women than men would sacrifice their own career for the partner. In reality I think the imbalance is even greater.

Moreover women with families or with elderly or sick relatives dependant on them are unable to benefit in their own interest from this 'freedom of movement'.

(iii) Employment/Unemployment

An EC prognosis (Cecchini-Report, 1988) says that after the completion of the Internal Market and after a short increase of unemployment in the next years around 7 mio new jobs will be created. That is supposed to be a signal of hope. I would like to draw attention to the fact that in the existing EC countries without East Germany there are around 16 mio officially recognised unemployed; the true total is certainly some mio higher. Female unemployment is higher than male unemployment in all countries, and I am afraid this will be our destiny as long as we have this system.

(iv) Women on the Labour Market

Economists and politicians of the European establishment are quick to contest the claim that women will be among the losers of 1992. They produce abundant statistical data of how women's employment situation has improved and argue that this proves women will profit even more than men from the new jobs offered in the EC.

What they do not mention is that much of the women's employment, both old and newly created, is of low quality. Local women's representatives, trade unionists and women politicians recently summed up the situation in my country: as the amount of female labour in the EC has increased, so has the proportion of contract work, unprotected work and home work. Statistics speak of women holding 60-90% of these positions.

Indeed, a growing part of the work in hotels and restaurants, retail shops and service enterprises is done under unprotected labour conditions, and most of these jobs are done by women. So-called normal working conditions have become the exception in newly created jobs for women, particularly in eastern and southern regions of our continent.

Employment statistics support this argument: between 1983 and 1988 the number of part-time jobs increased by 20% while the number of full-time jobs rose only 2%. This trend was confirmed by women from all EC countries.

Any analysis of the situation of women should be based not only on the situation of highly qualified women or those in secure positions, but also on the plight of shop assistants, cleaning women, migrant workers and homemakers who want or have to go back to paid work after rearing children.

An issue which I want to identify as particularly serious is the increasing exploitation of women doing contract work at home. Their numbers are increasing. I have brought with me a list 'A to Z' which self-help groups in the UK have compiled. Typically, this kind of labour is badly renumerated and often highly taxed. In countries like Portugal, for example, such women are regarded for tax purposes as self-employed.

We also find that the number of time-limited contracts has increased. The result is not only financial insecurity but also a considerable reduction of the ability of women and families concerned to plan their own lives.

The gap between qualified and unqualified women-workers is

widening, and the burdens on women who work increase rather than diminish. This negative assessment of the situation was shared by women from EC-member countries and from EFTA countries in a joint meeting. This draws our attention to the fact that the free market economy creates the same problems wherever its principles are being applied. The Internal Market reinforces them, and as my Finnish colleague pointed out some years ago; there is the danger that small non-EC countries are forced to their knees or to joining. How right she was!

Many of these developments are not specifically related to women but are rather negative for them. For instance, the separation between full-time employees on the one hand and people working part-time or on time-limited contracts on the other is in effect a division between protected and less protected workers. Within a company, this increases competition and lack of solidarity. We speak of de-solidarising structures being deliberately created in this and other instances. The use of part-time workers often increases a firm's output because such workers, with their shorter work hours, produce comparatively more. That norm of productivity may in turn be applied to full-time workers, who will not protest the higher expectations for fear of being dismissed.

Some economists project an increase of up to 35% in productivity. That will of course be profitable for the employers. But the men and women concerned will endanger their health while keeping the same salaries.

A particularly crass version of this is what is called in German Kapovaz—'capacity-oriented variable worktime'. Under this system —and I hear it is spreading rapidly in all countries—increasingly used in retail shops, a woman must always be on call to come in and work (for instance at peak sales times in department stores), but is of course paid only for the hours she actually works.

Under the heading 'Deregulation' there has been a watering down or removal of laws which served as protection for and to preserve the quality of life of the dependent employee. These were achievements of the Trade Union movements, belonging to a responsible social policy and until now considered as an assured component of our culture. I will just give a few headings:

- unprotected limited or short term work, chain contracts
- threat to the free week-end; Saturday as a regular workday; attack on the Sunday

  - sub contracted labour
  - Increase of shift work, longer shifts

For the most part women and men are both affected by this deregulation; women, however, to a much higher percentage than men. And it does not only make their working life difficult, but has negative effects on their old age social security. The employers policy of deregulation—often backed up by conservative governments—will increase the feminisation of poverty, or to put it more bluntly: the pauperisation of women.

Perhaps it will be surprising to learn that these negative developments have not been intended by the Treaty of Rome (1957). Right from the beginning the intention has been expressed to promote the economic and the social well-being of the people. In its preamble, the Treaty of Rome states that the Community's main goal is to guarantee social progress in its member countries and to strive for a continuing improvement of the living and working conditions of its people. But it is a fact that the 'social dimension' has been neglected over decades, and even when the new concept of a 'Single European Market' was developed and the Single European Act was agreed, the social dimension was again forgotten.

At a later stage we shall have to talk about the Community Charter of Fundamental Social Rights of Workers. Now I would just like to underline that powerful economic corporations and other lobby groups increasingly influence politics. It is a fact that economy rules politics and determines the priorities. Repeatedly we hear of powerful lobbies and national governments preventing the implementation of directives and recommendations to suit their interests.

Equal Treatment of Men and Women

Turning now to the specific question of the equality of men and women we find that the EC seems to be more progressive than most of its national members. This positive development, however, in the first place was not started out of a special respect for women, but again it was for competition's sake. France interfered right in the beginning of the then EEC. Not having such wage discrimination of women as the other countries the French government complained its employers would be put at a disadvantage if the other countries were allowed to continue their wage discriminating practices. Therefore Art.

119 was included in the Treaty of Rome. In later years it was the European Court of Justice applying the paragraph on the equal treatment of men and women to all areas of female employment which gradually brought about some positive measures for women, such as equal treatment in getting access to employment, training, and promotion. Up to now 5 Directives have passed the Council. They include questions of social security for women, social systems on company level, including provisions made for retirement allowances by the employers. (I apologise for incorrect language, but I had no access to English texts.)

From a legal point of new it is agreed that the EC Directives are more precise than for instance the German anti-discrimination legislation, and they have opened up a more comprehensive discussion on the matter of direct and indirect discrimination.

Downward Harmonisation

One problem now showing up draws our attention to the problematic side of the principle of equality. The European Court of Justice decided that Community Member States cannot ban night work for women. In response to the intervention of MEPs, Ms Papandreou, Commissioner for Social Affairs, stated that the provisions of the Treaty of Rome on equal treatment but 'absolutely be respected', and that, for this reason, the Member States which ban night work for women were asked to comply with the Court ruling before the end of February 1992 (France, Belgium, Italy, Spain, Portugal and Greece).

On 28 February agence Europe informed:

> This week, France, followed several hours later by Belgium, Spain, Greece, Italy and Portugal, denounced the International Labour Office (ILO) Convention which has banned night work for women since 1948. Today no Community Member State continues to apply this Convention to which neither Germany nor the United Kingdom had belonged .... The ILO nevertheless adopted, in 1990, a new Convention which aims at improving the living conditions of night workers. It urges the States to ratify it as soon as possible.

As the Information sheet 'Europe' reported on Friday 20 March 1992, several MEPs expressed the fear that if the countries in question repeal provisions banning night work for women, a legal void may be created paving the way to all kinds of abuse. A Belgium EMP recalled that the Parliament has expressed a view in principle against night work. He recalled that, according to a recent survey of workers in a Ford factory, only 10% of women polled favour night work. Mrs Papandreou replied that equality between men and women obviously implies that the disadvantages must be accepted along with the benefits.

She then mentioned that certain draft directives designed to take account of the particular situation of women are blocked in the Council, such as the one on parental leave. The directive on pregnant women is in the second reading stage.

I think we would agree with many of our colleagues that in the case of night work it would be more responsible to ban it for women and men. this, of course, raises the fundamental and burning question about 'downward harmonisation'. Apart from the legal approach of the European Court it is the declared aim of the employers to eliminate everything that could impede upon their competitiveness, and that means 'downward harmonising', although governments have been encouraged to maintain their social standards and rather harmonise 'upward' where there are deficits.

I should mention the fact the the Commission has launched three Action Programmes in order to promote the chances of women in the field of information and exchanges, raising public awareness of equality issues, vocational training, more justice in tax matters, and financial promotion for the creation of companies whose management positions and employee jobs are for the most part filled by women.

As I mentioned before the Council does bloc certain initiatives of the Commission in favour of women. On the other hand it has passed a recommendation to promote positive anti-discrimination measures. But the question is how national governments will react. Here is a very important field for our lobbying and intervening. There is very little democratic control of the EC's policy on the supranational level. But at least on the national level we should exercise it.

10

An Edinburgh
Case-Study

SUSAN HART

The movement towards equality of opportunity for women in employment is slow, peppered with many hurdles and setbacks. However, the purpose of this short essay is to highlight one example of good policy and practice in Scotland against the background of a mainly disinterested government and to look towards the potential of European developments.

I use the example of Edinburgh District Council's employment policies for women, as this large employer currently holds the title of ' ... the best employer for women in Scotland', according to a recent survey. The equal opportunities policies in the Council which afford them this distinction were developed over a seven year period after the acceptance of the argument (by some) that women Council workers did not have equality of opportunity and were not equally represented in senior positions. The effect of this, was reflected in the unequal service delivery to women members of the public.

The employment policies cover a variety of flexible working practices designed to recruit and retain skilled women workers and have been developed alongside policies for black and ethnic minority workers as well as those with disabilities. They include good management practices advocated over a number of years by many trade unions, women's groups voluntary organisations and community groups. Non discriminatory practices in the recruitment and selection of new workers have been set out in detail as has the training of staff in this field. Maternity leave (up to 22 weeks), paternity leave (up to 5 days), dependants leave (five days per year), job sharing, provision of a workplace nursery, sexual and racial harassment policies as well as access programmes for people with disabilities, combine to make Edinburgh District Council a very attractive employer. A career break scheme, offering up to two years unpaid leave with a guaranteed job to return to is also currently in the pipeline.

However, before we get carried away by the rosy glow that things are looking up for some women workers it must be pointed out that attitudes have not yet caught up with policy. A change in the culture and thinking of a still predominantly white, male institution has yet to come about from both management and workers. Recently a letter to the local newspaper from a male ex-employee of the Council complained about the lack of promotion opportunity—'women are taking our jobs out of pure greed' he stated angrily, highlighting very clearly the still massive prejudice that exists towards women workers.

Additionally, even with the implementation of the policies described, women employees of the Council are still concentrated in the lowest paid and low status jobs, *eg* clerical assistants, cleaners, telephonists *etc*. Requests for flexible childcare for school age children, a minimum wage, good quality training, safe and affordable transport and a host of other changes can clearly not be tackled by individual employers. These must be the responsibility of government. Changing workplace values to take account of the need of the individual outside the workplace, whether parents, carers or single people, not only requires changes in attitude and policy but also appropriately directed resources. Government action in this area has been sadly lacking and in the case of the proposed national minimum wage, positively hostile.

In terms of UK legislation, the Sex Discrimination Act (1975) and the Equal Pay Act have both provided useful case law in the battle against sex discrimination, but to take up a case or claim can be complex and lengthy to pursue, normally impossible for an individual acting on their own behalf. Very many women are discouraged from using this legislation, particularly as they have to bear the burden of proof.

Developments in Europe

In Europe, sex discrimination is only prohibited in certain distinct areas but this has not prevented the European court from developing a sophisticated and highly influential body of case law on the subject which in turn assists those women who have enough stamina and assistance, usually from their trade unions or the Equal Opportunities Commission, to take their employers or the government to court over sex discrimination.

Further developments in Europe are very uncertain. Based on the experience of the last ten years, very few proposals for binding EEC laws except for health and safety have been adopted. This is mainly due to the opposition of the UK to initiatives giving workers more rights—notably in the area of child care and temporary and part time workers, the majority of whom are low paid women. Some of the initiatives were resurrected under the guise of the Social Charter (now the Social Chapter of the Maastricht Treaty), potentially a statement of fundamental rights which could have improved living and working conditions in Europe so that the highest standards could be applied throughout the internal market. The Social Charter was agreed by eleven member states in 1989 but the UK Government did not accept it and it therefore has no legal force.

On a more positive note, the Directive from Europe on the protection of pregnant women has been agreed, albeit in a watered down version, again because the UK Government would not support the original. It gives women the right to 14 weeks maternity leave on pay no less than statutory sick pay (the original was for full pay), protection against dismissal and protection for the health and safety of pregnant women and those who have just given birth.

It is worth noting that the Social Charter made no mention whatsoever of the rights of black workers. Black women workers suffer a double discrimination in employment in Scotland, as in the rest of Europe and this should give us all cause for concern, particularly in the light of the deliberate fuelling of racial hatred by far right political parties and groupings across Europe whose activities are on the increase and seem to be gaining some support. The UK Race Relation Act does go some way towards giving protection to black workers in this country, however, as with the Sex Discrimination Act, there is a definite need for strengthening the legislation and the widespread adoption by employers of policies dealing with racial harassment. These measures are not supported by the present UK Government and are unlikely to be developed by the European Community when some countries have been promoting racist policies intended to restrict the movement of black workers across Europe.

Racism and fear of job losses must be tackled by the trade union movement to ensure there is no collusion by predominantly white workforces to discriminatory practices by employers. Links, networking and campaigns across Europe on issues concerning black women must be developed and supported. Similarly, appropriate and effective policies to ensure that the problems facing developing countries are neither ignored nor increased by a strengthened Europe.

The uncertainty over the future of the Maastricht Treaty, including the social aspects of it clearly begs the question of whether or not we can rely solely on European developments to improve the position of women workers. An acceptance in this country of the need for attitudinal changes in the way employers. government, trade unions and the general public view the needs of individual workers and families would be the most powerful fulcrum for change. We can view European developments, such as the strengthening of EC social legislation as a helpful factor in forcing changes in the UK as well as raising expectations amongst workers for improvements, however it is no substitute for the empowerment of women workers through education, campaigning and participation in democratic processes, both at work and in the community.

The trade union movement, women's groups, community groups and the political parties all have a role to play, campaigning on issues such as improved childcare provision, introduction of a minimum wage, job sharing, maternity and paternity leave and a variety of other equal opportunities measures. Changes in the workplace must also go hand in hand with changes in the home if women are to have true equality of opportunity. Men must share equally in the burden of childcare and other domestic responsibilities, but that is a topic for another book!

11

Developing an
Equal Opportunities Policy
in ICI Pharmaceuticals

SUE PURVES

In many organisations job adverts which make claims that 'we are an equal opportunities employer' are greeted with cynicism. After all this is the law. For the employer and manager it offers a vast challenge in terms of the vision it encapsulates and the practices required to reach it. What do we have to do differently to reach this goal? Is it okay if I treat everyone equally as a matter of course? How do we recognise it when we get there?—these are all questions which baffle those who are used to managing change in their technical fields.

For a business in the chemical industry the target looks forbidding; here our typical employee might be perceived to be a male science graduate, and those in the most senior roles are typically graduates of the 1950s and 60s when few women read science, and even fewer went into the private sector. It is thus important to seek improvement targets which the business and its employees consider to be important, rather than to reach out and embrace all the goals which are suggested by the national debates.

The most important step is to gather data which helps to define and pinpoint specific areas for improvement in ensuring that our employment policies maximise the contributions which al employees, men and women can make to the business. Our sources of data included our employment statistics, including those for gender of job applicants and those who succeeded, leavers, promotions, numbers on maternity leave and numbers returning. These provide the most potent data for convincing colleagues that there are areas for improvement. In addition we had data from an international ICI task force which studied the working practices of international businesses considered to be at the 'leading edge' in the equal opportunities field; from a detailed questionnaire sent to all women who left the business during a period of two years; from a project carried out by a graduate student to elicit male and female perceptions of the organisation, and from a questionnaire which all employees were invited to complete concerning child care arrangements.

Our data suggested:

Men and women identified and sought the same improvements in the way they were managed. They wanted to know more about the progress of the business, and the contribution which they cold make to its success. They wanted more prioritisation of their workload, and they expected good feedback about the progress they were making.

Most parents felt that they had made adequate child care arrangements, and their choices were varied. What all had in common was the worry of making arrangements for child care when the minder was sick, after school and in the holidays.

The international study suggested that other companies found that legislation and equal opportunities policies raised awareness, but did not bring about change, better family care policies (maternity pay, creche *etc*) were greatly appreciated but left unresolved issues of management practice, and in some cases encouraged the feeling that women were different and more difficult to employ. Significant progress could only be made when 'managing difference' was acknowledged to be a key managerial skill at the very heart of business processes. The key areas where managers needed to be aware of differences between people was in the way they judged success, and developed their people's careers. Manager's success in this area would be judged in the outcomes of the career development process.

This data was critical to the strategy we adopted to foster equal opportunities in ICI Pharmaceuticals. The responsibility for managing and developing each individual employee effectively lay with the line manager, and the key process for achieving this lay in the setting of objectives for each work team and targets for each individual, in the quarterly performance review discussion and in the creation and updating of individual development plans. Here managers needed to be sensitive about the judgements which they made on individuals. Evidence suggests that men and women work in different ways and this must be taken into account in making judgments about how goals were achieved.

The outcomes of each individual process are summarised for each function's career development group Each group was invited to set appropriate targets to ensure that it was not overlooking the development needs of the women in the team. These targets are not quotas; they are the outcome of discussions amongst the group about what would be appropriate. They may take the form of listing women of potential and monitoring their career development moves on an annual basis, or identifying the number of promotions which women might be expected to achieve on the basis of the data available, or setting retention targets *etc.* The key issue here is to set in train some process of target setting and reflection, so that where goals are not achieved managers can make proposals for improvement. As a final stage in the process each business is required to report on progress in developing women at the ICI annual succession review with each business.

One aspect of our policy to facilitate the developments of women has been to improve our policies to help parents with young families. During 1991 ICI improved its maternity leave arrangements, offering the equivalent of full salary for the period that State maternity benefit is payable, to those women who return after maternity leave. Women may take maternity leave for up to a total of 52 weeks, or may make a gradual return to full-time employment. In addition ICI operates a Career Break scheme to enable men and women time away from their careers, for family reasons.

Our efforts to develop arrangements for child care have met with several difficulties. Our data suggested that employees had quite differing needs of child care in terms of the facilities they required, location and cost. The care and concern they showed for choosing a school for their child was far outweighed by the care and concern they exhibited in choosing child care. For a business trying to be supportive of their needs this was a potential minefield. Our strategy has been to work with other employers to encourage a variety of new off-site facilities in differing locations, and to sponsor the development of stay-late and holiday play activities. We decided against a workplace nursery for a variety of reasons, including its selectivity in terms of the numbers it could accommodate and those able to take advantage because of their ability to pay, its start-up and aftercare costs, and the inappropriateness of encouraging commuting infants. A minority of our employees regret this decision, although neighbouring employers who have opted to provide the facility identify with many of the issues which we highlighted.

Perhaps our outstanding success in the area of child care has been in the sheer creativity which managers have used to enable parents with specific child care issues to combine career and family. For example, flexible return to work after maternity leave is now the norm, and there is a special evening shift in the factory to enable experienced quality assurers to work on a flexible weekly basis. Excellent job share arrangements abound. This is line management of individuals at its very best.

One of the unexpected outcomes of our approach was the 'credibility gap' which developed. As awareness was raised, so were expectations of dramatic change. Instead change has been gradual but positive, and the outcome of many individual management decisions. As a result many women questioned the sincerity with which we implemented the policy, but remained reticent to challenge managers because they feared that they would be seen as 'trouble makers'. The task has been to persuade the women and their senior managers to discuss the issue together so that managers could demonstrate their bias for action and at the same time persuade the women concerned that they too had their part to play. These processes are now taking place and they have had a very positive impact on key male and female opinion leaders in the business; and we must seek to ensure that this process is continued. The next step is to increase managerial competence in leading diverse groups of people; in getting them to recognise difference and manage different people differently. To this end we are preparing a training module for all managers as part of our performance management training.

In addition a group of women of potential are making recommendations to the business about the components of a training and development strategy for equal opportunities. Those include developing management training modules on 'managing diversity', providing a check-list for managers to help with the implementation of Equal Opportunities, and promoting mentoring.

We work in a business culture which emphasises results, and we shall need to show progress in improving our employment statistics concerning women. In the area of equal opportunities we are seeking to change management practices and attitudes. We thus expect much of the change to be subtle and difficult to measure on a short time scale. Nevertheless the large increase in flexible working practices, and the increased representation of women in more senior grades are tangible measure of our progress.

12
Royal Dutch Shell Company Ltd
DONALD M ROSS
and HUGH C ORMISTON

Company Commitment
to Equal Opportunities for Women

Shell is a company participating in the Government's 'Opportunity 2000' scheme. The company likes to be thought of as a leader in the field of equal opportunities, basing its claim on its 15 year old company philosophy and its steadfast pursuit of equal opportunities policies over at least this period of time. While the company has firmly set its face against any policies of positive discrimination, preferring to base promotion entirely upon merit, nevertheless it has instituted maternity policies, career break schemes, recruitment policies, flexible working policies and specific forms of training for women, in an effort to promote its overall objective of equal opportunities. In addition, it has for some years now been separately monitoring the progress of women within the company, and has a substantial statistical database, specifically on its female employees, in parallel with databases for the labour force as a whole.

The Arguments in Favour

Shell recognises that increasing competition means that no company can afford to ignore the pool of high quality female labour which is available. The company frankly admits it is this basic economic consideration which drives their equal opportunities programme:

> If British businesses are to stay competitive they have to make it attractive for women to work for them, and that means giving them a fair deal in recruitment, training and promotion. The reason is simple: the pool from which employers can draw good quality and well qualified male employees is shrinking, and they

must make the most of the untapped reservoir of talent that women can offer.

This is the crux of how Shell views equal opportunities: as a business objective, just as valid as reaching production targets or achieving high quality standards. The view is that the company needs certain skills that are in short supply; women are an under-used source of those skills, therefore they are a resource to be fully developed.

While Shell is reluctant to speak of a particular management style, and prefers instead to speak of a mixture of management styles, at the same time they recognise that there are some underlying shifts in management philosophy which appear to be more permanent that mere changes of fashion. They recognise that the contemporary emphasis on teamwork may fall into this category, and here again, for economic reasons, women are a resource that can no longer be ignored:

> The new thrust of putting equal opportunities policies into action aims to recognise that assessing women's potential may need a different approach from that traditionally used. The challenge is to understand where this is needed to make the most of the different qualities that men and women can bring to business.

When the subject was discussed during a syndicate session on leadership and management style during a recent management conference, it was felt that having more women in management could bring a different perspective. Shell Expro personnel director Jerry Saville, who led the session, says:

> It is my personal view, though there is evidence to back it up, that women often bring a different dimension to team-building and getting commitment from others.
> There are many styles of management and it would be foolish not to exploit the best. Studies show that, generally speaking, en behave in a transactional way—they like to do a deal. Women persuade people, in a transformational way. Though at first glance the first approach might seem stronger, in today's organisations with the emphasis on teamwork, the second may be more effective.
> At the very least, it would give us a spread of management styles, and people could widen their own range by seeing others

in action. Managing the business is not enough; our most important asset is people, and we have to manage them effectively to get the best from them.

Culture Change?

At the same time, Shell recognises that the problem of equal opportunities is also a problem of attitude change and that this is an area where the company is part of a wider culture that has arguably discriminated against women for centuries. In practice, it is said, that when a busy manager is short of an engineer, for example, his first concern is to get hold of a suitable engineer rather than to ask the question, will that person be male or female? There is also a tacit admission that some managers may be incapable now of changing their approach to equal opportunities policies. Indeed, Shell claim to have a decentralised management style which devolves authority to individual managers and makes it more difficult for the company to impose a uniform corporate strategy in this regard.

> Shell has been described as a paternalistic company, especially in the past, and its activities are in traditionally male fields where ability has been assessed on traditionally male premises. The company is now questioning whether this tends to downgrade the qualities that women can bring to the workplace, putting them at an unfair disadvantage.
> 'There are so many views on why women haven't got on; attitudes in society and attitudes at work are inextricably linked,' says Chris Marsh. 'Are policies formed as a result of changing attitudes, or do the policies force the change? It's probably a bit of both. What we're interested in is looking forward and seeing how we can make real progress.'

In this regard Shell claim to have a company cultural advantage. Within the company there has always been less emphasis on the individual compared to other oil companies, and more emphasis on the collective effort of the company as a whole. It claims always to have taken a long-term view of its activity, even at the expense of being perhaps a little less profitable than some of its competitors. Unlike some more expansive companies it has not had to absorb very different company cultures in recent years, but has been able to build slowly and firmly on the culture which has evolved since the inception of the company.

Why do more Women leave than Men?

One aspect of employing women which has concerned the company has been the higher rate of turnover for women compared to men:

We have a duty to argue on the facts. One of the facts is that Shell seems to lose its women graduates in greater numbers than the men. The figures are not huge, but it is significant that of each year's intake a greater proportion of the women resign than men. It is pointless recruiting people if you lose them quickly.

Studies have been carried out among undergraduates to explore career aspirations and perceptions of various industries and companies, as a way of discovering misconceptions about industry. These also help to show how Shell's image as an employer matches students' needs; also how it compares with that of other companies. Research is also going on currently to chart the careers of graduates who joined Shell between 1983 and 1990, to pinpoint significant difference in progression rates, according to various categories.

As part of their concern to hold on to women employees, Shell's maternity policy is one of the best of any company. Women get 6 months maternity pay, half at the beginning of their leave and the rest paid in stages during the first 9 months after they return to work.

The company's career break scheme, which allows people, men and women, to take two or three years out from work to care for children, has not been widely taken up. In the first place, it applies only to people deemed by management and personnel to have a longer rather than a shorter term future with the company. Candidates may. of course, be reluctant to make use of the career break scheme for fear of prejudicing future career prospects and, of course, because they could not cope with the loss of income. The company also admits that its flexible working policies have not been very successful. Few employees engage in job sharing and few are on part-time working schemes.

Some 150 women within the company have, however, taken part in the training scheme geared for upwardly mobile women to enable them to cope with a company culture which is recognised to have been male dominated since its inception.

This year (1992) Shell in Aberdeen hope to establish a nursery for children of employees. Nevertheless with this project the company may find they are not meeting the expectations of women, which have moved on from nurseries to kindergartens where children are not simply 'minded', but enabled to develop as they would with a mother at home. Consequently, Shell may find that they are under pressure both to change the word 'nursery' for their projected scheme in Aberdeen and, more importantly, to rethink the content of the project.

Shell employee, Aimee Brinzer, not only underlines the importance of child care facilities but tellingly records the difference that having a family makes for women compare to men:

> I don't think it is easy for women because it is male dominated, so facilities like child-care are not there. The most difficult issue for women is children, and it's a choice men don't have to make. In fact for a man it's a bonus; a family means he is seen as steady and responsible. For a woman, it's seen as a significant disadvantage.

Company Objectives

Shell are indicating the seriousness with which they take this issue by publishing a number of targets and associated action plans. These include increasing the 'proportion of women recruited so that they match the relevant skill pool for each job, where they are currently under-represented.' The action proposed includes undertaking 'positive action' recruitment advertising, monitoring every stage of each individual campaign, and providing equal opportunities good practice for everyone involved in recruitment.

The second target is 'to improve retention rates of female employees', recognising that in 1991, 197 men resigned, *ie* 2% of the male employees, whereas 101 women resigned, representing 4.8% of female employees. The actions proposed to achieve the target include encouraging the use of flexible working arrangements, ensuring appropriate support is available for all staff on maternity leave, *eg* running a returner's workshop, and conducting in-depth exit interviews for all leavers.

A further target is 'to increase the percentage of women in the management cadre each year'. At the end of 1991 there were 330 women in management positions, representing 9% of the total. Actions associated with this target include maintaining commitment to choosing the best person for the job in all selection processes, including a woman candidate on job shortlists wherever suitably qualified candidates are available, supporting women-only training, and monitoring the development of staff to ensure there is no sex differentiation in their treatment.

Finally, the company aims 'to raise the awareness of equal opportunities among all staff, and to communicate policies, action plans and successes, both internally and to the wider community'. It hopes to achieve this by providing awareness training for staff and communicating commitment to ensuring that equal opportunity is recognised as an integral part of good management. It hopes to promote role models, to communicate commitment to equal opportunity to prospective recruits in schools and colleges, and to make sure that recruitment agencies supplying staff act in accordance with it.

13

Home Truths
about Homeworking

DIAN LEPPINGTON

In December 1988, Bernadette Kendell from Calderdale, gave the
following testimony as part of a delegation organised by the European
Network of Women to the European Parliament:

I am an ex-outworker. When I did outwork, I used to make
Christmas crackers. All in all, it took roughly three minutes to make
one. They consisted of six to a box and I was paid one penny per
cracker. I earned roughly 40 pence an hour. I also made gift tags,
which consisted of six tags, three green, three red, one red ribbon
and one green ribbon. I folded them all, put them all in bags and
was given one penny per bag.

There was many a time I used to stay up all night so as to get my
wage packet at the end of the week, for buying shoes, clothes and
sometimes food, for my children. Many people thought I did this for
leisure money. But this was not the case. I did this to buy things
which were a necessity.

I could not go out to work because I have small children. So I
got them to bring work to me. I used to put in 90 hours a week. There
would be boxes stacked everywhere—little toys, paper hats and
mottoes all over the room. The paper was so dazzling that my eyes
used to hurt and then would come the headaches, followed by a
migraine. I would get terrible backache. But I could not stop for fear
of losing some of my wages.

Then it dawned on me that I wasn't gaining anything from all
this work because of all the gas and electricity I was using and I
couldn't work faster or harder than I already was. I was so upset
when I realised I was doing all this work for nothing. In fact, at the end
of the week they probably owed me money for fuel.

Anyway, I have stopped all that now and started my own group
to try and help all the people that might be in the same position as I
was. My heart goes out to these women because I know just what
they are going through and how hard these must work sometimes
to survive.

The turning point for Bernie was a public meeting in Bradford in June 1988. This meeting was a joint initiative of Leeds Industrial Mission and the Yorkshire and Humberside Low Pay Unit, to which we invited homeworkers, community workers and people from local authority departments from all over West Yorks in order to found a West Yorkshire Homeworking Group.

With her friend Karen, and Lorna a local community worker, Bernie got together a group on her housing estate, on a bleak hill side above Halifax. They drew up a leaflet and distributed copies from house to house. The following year for them was largely spent joggling the demands of family life—both Bernie and Karen were mothers of small children—whilst they became almost full time campaigners.

The climax of the campaign came when their local MP, Alice Mason, named Woolworth in the House of Commons as a firm which was marketing Christmas cars packed by Calderdale homeworkers, at a rate of pay which the homeworkers themselves estimated worked out at below 50 pence an hour.

It should be said that, this particular case involved Woolworth, they are by no means the only 'household name' firm who are (indirectly) involved in this sort of exploitation. Mostly homeworkers do not know where their products are being sold, but it just so happened that in this particular case the pack of cards included a wrapper which said 'With all good wishes for Christmas and the New Year from Woolworth.'

In response to being 'named' at Westminster Woolworth immediately called a meeting with the homeworking group in Halifax to which they sent a team, including their Managing Director. And it was here that for the first time we encountered what we have subsequently found to be the standard line of argument from employers. First, they said they had not received any of the three letters which the homeworking group had sent to them. That was why they hadn't replied. Second, they claim that only a small proportion of their suppliers employed homeworkers (we're sceptical about this, but how can you prove it?) Third, they remarked that the homeworkers evidently didn't have nimble fingers, and that they ought to be able to produce far more in an hour. Fourth, they complained about the standard of their work.

The upshot of all the resulting publicity vividly illustrates the inherent problems of campaigning on this sort of issue. The subcontractors who had been supplying the work simply disappeared, and now it is presumably done elsewhere. For those like Bernie who'd decided that the work was just not worth doing anyway this was not a loss, but there were of course many other homeworkers on the estate who still wanted it. There was also a lot of anger on the estate at the television program which was made, featuring the group. Many of the neighbours were very unhappy seeing the estate portrayed in what they considered a somewhat unflattering light. Bernie has since left the area.

It appears that West Yorkshire is a major national centre for the Christmas card and cracker industry. But that is by no means the only sort of homework we have come across. On the contrary we have found over a hundred different types of homework including such things: ambulance kit bags (sewing); arran sweaters (knitting); budgie cages (assembling parts); peeling onions/brussel sprouts (48 pound sacks); burglar alarms; board games; book indexing; curtain rails (packing); computer leads (assembly); first aid kits (filling); light sockets, lobster pots ....

The great majority of these workers are women. Contrary to widespread assumptions it is not peculiarly a feature of the Asian community.

The work is almost always paid on a piece rate system. A survey of homeworkers in Calderdale indicated that the average estimated hourly rate of pay was £1.17 per hour. A similar survey carried out in Leeds revealed a figure of £1.16 per hour, remarkably close to the average pay received by the Calderdale women.

Pay Rates in Bands

Hourly Rate	Number of Homeworkers
below 50 pence	17
50p – 99p	4
£1.00 – 1.49	12
£1.50 – 1.99	7
£2.00 – 2.49	4
£2.50 – 2.99	2
£3.00	4
Total	50

Homeworkers usually lack any health and safety provision, or employment rights such as holiday, sickness pay or any reimbursement of expenses: electricity, gas bills: the cost of buying and servicing a sewing or knitting machine *etc*. Their homes become both the work place and the warehouse, often filled with large boxes stacked to the ceiling. Many women fell they have no option but to be homeworkers, in order to supplement the income of very low paid partners or income support and as a way of combing employment with the care of children or other dependants. But it is not easy to work with children clamouring for attention, so many work late into the night. Often homes are filled with the relentless whirring of machines—also a hazard for small children. Some products involve dangerous solvents, other sorts of work involving large quantities of fabric dust leads to bronchial problems. Perhaps worse of all, as one homeworker put it: I'm stuck in the house all week. There's no work mates. I miss the company of others ... Janine. When someone is working for such low wages there is very little time for social activity.

It is impossible to say how many such homeworkers there are in Britain because no accurate figures are kept. But on the basis of our research, partly information from employers and concentrated work on certain housing estates, we guess that there are probably somewhere between 5000-10,000 homeworkers in the city of Leeds alone. In general, one of the great problems with homeworking is its hidden nature.

One day the Homeworking Group received a phone call from a young woman in one of the outlying parts of Leeds who told us that she hadn't been paid for packing 90,000 Christmas tags (non-payment is very common), and she didn't know the name of the supplier or how to get in touch with them (the work was simply delivered by a van driver). The problem was she was moving house. The boxes took up a lot of space. Was she legally obliged to take them with her? Subsequent investigation revealed that other people had not been paid for doing similar work. And none of them knew who the supplier was either. But someone reported seeing large stacks of boxes, bearing the same logo, in a nearby garden guarded by rott-weilers. It turned out that this house was a centre for a network of about fifty people all doing the same work.

We also identified the logo on the boxes, as belonging to a major producer of charity Christmas cards. So this led us to get in touch with the charities concerned. The charities directed us to their national advisory council; the advisory council contacted the middleman between themselves and the card manufacturers; the middleman contacted the manufacturer; and the manufacturer put pressure on the sub-contractors; who in turn were sub-contracting to the house with rottweilers. Eventually they paid up.

However, it also seemed disturbing to the homeworking group that charities were involved, even at so many removes, in a process involving homeworkers who were in fact being paid at rates of well below 50 pence an hour. This was not the fault of the sub-contractors, who were themselves only just managing to keep their heads above water. The card manufacturer, on the other hand, were a multimillionaire paid enterprise.

Unfortunately, we were not able to persuade the charities themselves that there was any serious problems here. But we did manage to enter into negotiations with the Bradford based manufacturer. And when they learned that a Yorkshire Television program was being made about our work, they agreed to instruct their sub-contractors that the rates of pay for Christmas cards, in particular, should from now on not be less that £2.00 per hour—a massive pay rise, in theory! Unfortunately, this has only meant that the Christmas tag and card work has been withdrawn from the estate. Again the same dilemma.

Has it all been worth it? It certainly seems that without government legislation there can be no improvements in the economic circumstances of homeworkers. And even where there is good legislation, and there is in Italy, experience shows that it is very hard to implement. Nor do we think there would be any gain in the abolition of homework.

Certainly the West Yorkshire Homeworking Group has contributed something of value to a number of people. It has helped bring homeworkers out of their isolation, it's been very important to be able to swap their stories with one another. A major part of our work has involved organising things like day trips to the seaside and the pantomime, family holidays for people who otherwise scarcely leave their estate. It has been a process of building trust between neighbours who are often very suspicious of one another beforehand—homeworking breeds fear because people often think, sometimes wrongly—that they are not supposed to use their homes as work places.

For those homeworkers, or ex-homeworkers who have been centrally involved in the actual running of the group the experience has also been a liberating one. People have discovered abilities they never dreamed they had. It has been an eye opener for all of us—

and not least through the international contacts we've developed: in particular with homeworkers and projects in The Netherlands, Portugal, India and the Philippines.

And perhaps justice here, is not only a matter of pay and working conditions, in themselves, vital though it is that these must be improved. There is also the issue of recognition. Homeworkers make a significant contribution to the British economy, and yet it is a contribution which remains largely hidden. The struggle to make public the way things are is at the same time to affirm the dignity of those who are trapped, often in such demeaning circumstances. That is why it is important for the church to be involved. This is a group of people completely outside the scope of trade union activity, with no political clout, whose voices in the natural run of things would never be heard; which in itself is a form of poverty.

It is a question of people stepping out of the shadows to become real participants in the world, truth tellers from a perspective that is mostly obscured. And is not the truth, also, part of the wealth of nations?

Bibliography

The following publications are either referred to in the text of this report or contain useful background information:

West Yorkshire Homeworking Group: *A Penny a Bag*, Yorkshire and Humberside Low Pay Unit, 1990. A report on the first eighteen months of the work of the Homeworking Group.

A Survey of Homeworking in Calderdale, Yorkshire and Humberside Low Pay Unit, July 1991. A report on a six month study of homeworking (outworking) in Calderdale.

Outworkers' News, newsletter of the West Yorkshire Homeworking Group. It contains news of the activities of the group and is available free to homeworkers.

Yorkshire and Humberside Low Pay Unit Newsletter contains articles on homeworking.

Sheila Allen and Carol Wolkowitz: *Homeworking: Myths and Realities*, Macmillan Education, 1987.

Social Protection of Homeworkers, Documents of the Meeting of Experts on the Social Protection of Homeworkers, International Labour Office, Geneva, 1990.

The Protection of Persons Working at Home, Report prepared by the Study Group of the 1987/1988 Co-ordinated Social Research

Programme, Council of Europe, Strasbourg 1989.

Jane Tate: *Homework in Europe,* paper for the Working Group on Economic and Social Cohesion, November 1991.

Mary Hopkins: *Training Courses for Homeworkers,* School of Policy Studies, Cranfield Institute of Technology, Cranfield, Bedford, MK43 OA1, October 1989.

Homeworking in Birmingham—A Report of the Ad Hoc Officer Working Group on Homeworking, Birmingham City Council, 1988.

Outwork in Leeds—A Report by the West Yorkshire Homeworking Group, March 1992.

14

Together in Unison

A Case Study
in Union Development

The New Union—Together in Unison

At the time of this publication going to press, a most significant development is taking place within three of the major trade union organisations in Britain. COHSE, NALGO and NUPE have produced final proposals for an amalgamation of the three unions to form a New Union for workers providing services to the public. The discussions have been careful, detailed and based upon wide consultation. However they recognise that prospects of creating a New Union is both difficult and exciting and they have endeavoured to respect the needs and traditions of each of the three partner unions and have sought to build upon them in their joint proposals. Compromise and accommodation has been necessary in each of the proposals they bring forward.

The prospect of creating this New Union, Unison, is seen by them and others as one of the most important developments in the British trade union movement.

The intention from the beginning was that the New Union would be flexible and structured so that it could anticipate and respond quickly to changes in its external environment and it was agreed that it should be open and accessible to all members and not simply to activists and also to the wider community. It is hoped that the New Union should be innovative and a force for reform and development in policy, service provision and trade union action. It was also accepted that its structure should be built from the membership upwards and that the whole approach would be member-centred. The three unions have agreed to three fundamental principles:

— A belief in the need for a renewal and revival of collective public provision.
— A commitment to a democratic, pluralist and a decentralised approach.

— The paramount importance of equal opportunities and fair
representation.

The following is abstracted from the final report of the 3 unions:

Equal Opportunities

None of this will be achieved overnight, and systematic progress
will require a range of initiatives at different levels of the New
Union. Thus, a clear commitment to the development of equal
opportunities and the achievement of fair representation must
be reflected in the New Union's aims and objects, rules, organisation and structure; and also in its various representative systems, bargaining agenda and strategies, education and training,
publicity and publications, and employment policies and practices. Action in each of these spheres at all levels amounts to a
big challenge and will take time and make demands on New
Union resources.

In all of this, it will be important to take initiatives so as to
win widespread support for them and, in so doing, to strengthen the
New Union as a whole. The pursuit of equal opportunities can
enhance union democracy and provide a better service to all
members. It can also lead to improved services to the wider
public by showing how these values should also be central to the
provision of services in a civilised society.

Fair representation will continue to be essential for the very
wide range of occupations, status, pay levels and positions which
members of the New Union will hold. Systems of representation
will need to reflect this diversity and provide opportunities for
all members.

Similarly the New Union should reflect the fact that two-thirds
of the members will be women. In some service groups and sectors
the proportion will be lower, in some higher. In each case, it should
be the aim to move towards proportional representation for
women. The timetable for proportionality should be no late than
the year 2000.

The proportion of women at each level and in each sphere of
the New Union should be ascertained.

Appropriate targets for proportionality should be agreed and an agreed timetable and mechanism for their achievement laid down. Where progress can be achieved earlier than the end of the century, this should be agreed.

Targets should cover the composition of all New Union committees, conferences, meetings and delegations, and should always bear in mind the need to make progress and avoid rigidity and excessive red tape.

Appropriate guidelines, training and education programmes should be established to win support for proportionality and assist its introduction.

Proportionality for women should be implemented alongside fair representation and women's self-organisation, and be subject to monitoring and review.

The aim should be to adopt proportionality progressively to increase the status and confidence of women and their access to responsibility, authority and power in the New Union. This should be done so as to strengthen the New Union as a whole and enrich participation by all members.

In some cases, as equal opportunities are established, and members feel able to gain access to representation and power in the New Union, some of the arrangements may become less necessary. Only time and a proper review of practice and experience will tell. In many cases, the aim has been to allow for flexible, and relatively informal self-organisation to be established. The aim is to stimulate and encourage; to build confidence and link members into the mainstream of New Union activity; and to empower them.

These structural arrangements will need to be complemented in other ways. The rules of the New Union will explicitly oppose racism, sexism, homophobia and discrimination against members on grounds of gender, sexuality, race, disability, religion or creed. Education and training programmes promoting equal opportunities and fair representation will be established for members, activists, lay officials and paid staff.

The literature, publicity and publications of the New Union will also need to reflect its commitment and programme for equal opportunities and fair representation. So will the union's own employment policies and practices. The union will need to expand its representation and campaigns in support of disadvantaged members. In particular, the needs and aspirations of women, black members, members with disabilities, lesbians and gay men will need to be reflect in the New Union's bargaining agenda and strategies.

Similarly, the central aims of fair representation, proportionality and self-organisation should always be borne in mind. They are to bring members into activity with the confidence to play their own part. Members should be able to benefit from the opportunities and resources available, and share in decision-making. The aim is neither to establish separate organisations, divorced from the mainstream arrangements, nor to create parallel structures which 'shadow' all the New Union's organisational arrangements.

Our aim is to provide access to the New Union, to make it truly representative of the spread of interest of its members and to involve them in decision-making and policy formulation; in short, to empower members at all levels. The arrangements and initiatives are also intended to improve members' situations at work, in the wider community and in their own lives. All these aims should be remembered when implementing policies and establishing structures and other support for equal opportunities in the New Union.

(i)   Equal opportunities and fair representation will be central to the New Union's organisation and structure at all levels.

(ii)   Proportionality for women has already been agreed. The objective is progressively to achieve proportional representation for women at all levels of the New Union by the end of the century.

(iii) Self-organisation for women, black members, lesbians and gay men and members with disabilities has already been agreed. Self-organisation will be able to operate at local and branch level, regional and national levels. The precise form of self-organisation will differ from group to group and location to location.

(iv)   Fair representation will be essential to achieve a fair and reasonable balance between the three partner unions and will need to reflect the diversity of occupations, status and pay levels of all members.

(v)   The New Union's National Executive together with regions will monitor and review all arrangements for fair representation, proportionality and self-organisation.

The Community Charter
of the Fundamental
Social Rights of Workers

THE HEADS OF STATE OR GOVERNMENT OF THE MEMBER
STATES OF THE EUROPEAN COMMUNITY MEETING AT
STRASBOURG ON 9 DECEMBER 1989.[1]

Whereas, under the terms of Article 117 of the EEC Treaty, the
Member States have agreed on the need to promote improved living
and working conditions for workers so as to make possible their
harmonization while the improvement is being maintained;

Whereas following on from the conclusions of the European Councils
of Hanover and Rhodes the European Council of Madrid considered
that, in the context of the establishment of the single European
market, the same importance must be attached to the social aspects
as to the economic aspects and whereas, therefore, they must be
developed in a balanced manner;

Having regard to the Resolutions of the European Parliament of 15
March 1989, 14 September 1989 and 22 November 1989, and to the
Opinion of the Economic and Social Committee of 22 February 1989;

Whereas the completion of the internal market is the most effective
means of creating employment and ensuring maximum well-being in
the Community; whereas employment development and creation
must be given first priority in the completion of the internal market;
whereas it is for the Community to take up the challenges of the
future with regard to economic competitiveness, taking into account,
in particular, regional imbalances;

Whereas the social consensus contributes to the strengthening of the
competitiveness of undertakings, of the economy as a whole and to the
creation of employment; whereas in this respect it is an essential
condition for ensuring sustained economic development;

Whereas the completion of the internal market must favour the approximation of improvements in living and working conditions, as well as economic and social cohesion within the European Community while avoiding distortions of competition;

Whereas the completion of the internal market must offer improvements in the social field for workers of the European Community, especially in terms of freedom of movement, living and working conditions, health and safety at work, social protection, education and training;

Whereas, in order to ensure equal treatment, it is important to combat every form of discrimination, including discrimination on grounds of sex, colour, race, opinions and beliefs, and whereas, in a spirit of solidarity, it is important to combat social exclusion;

Whereas it is for Member States to guarantee that workers from non-member countries and members of their families who are legally resident in a Member State of European Community are able to enjoy, as regards their living and working conditions, treatment comparable to that enjoyed by workers who are nations of the Member State concerned;

Whereas inspiration should be drawn from the Conventions of the International Labour Organization and from the European Social Charter of the Council of Europe;

Whereas the Treaty, as amended by the Single European Act, contains provisions laying down the powers of the Community relating *inter alia* to the freedom of movement of workers (Articles 7, 48 to 51), the right of establishment (Articles 52 to 58), the social field under the conditions laid down in Articles 117 to 122—in particular as regards the improvement of health and safety in the working environment (Article 118a), the development of the dialogue between management and labour at European level (Article 118b), equal pay for men and women for equal work (Article 119)—the general principles for implementing a common vocations training policy (Article 128), economic and social cohesion (Article 130a to 130e) and, more generally, the approximation of legislation (Article 100, 100a and 235); whereas the implementation of the Charter must not entail an extension of the Community's powers as defined by the Treaties;

Whereas the aim of the present Charter is on the one hand to consolidate the progress made in the social field, through action by the Member States, the two sides of industry and the Community;

Whereas its aim is on the other hand to declare solemnly that the implementation of the Single European Act must take full account of the social dimension of the Community and that it is necessary in this context to ensure at appropriate levels the development of the social rights of workers of the European Community, especially employed workers and self-employed persons;

Whereas in accordance with the conclusions of the Madrid European Council, the respective roles of Community rules, national legislation and collective agreements must be clearly established;

Whereas, by virtue of the principle of subsidiarity, responsibility for the initiatives to be taken with regard to the implementation of these social rights lies with the Member States or their constituent parts and, within the limits of its powers, with the European Community; whereas such implementation may take the form of laws, collective agreements or existing practices at the various appropriate levels and whereas it requires in many spheres the active involvement of the two sides of industry;

Whereas the solemn proclamation of fundamental social rights at European Community level may not, when implemented, provide grounds for any retrogression compared with the situation currently existing in each Member State.

HAVE ADOPTED THE FOLLOWING DECLARATION CONSTITUTING THE 'COMMUNITY CHARTER OF THE FUNDAMENTAL SOCIAL RIGHTS OF WORKERS':

Freedom of movement

1   Every worker of the European Community shall have the right to freedom of movement throughout the territory of the Community, subject to restrictions justified on grounds of public order, public safety or public health.

2   The right to freedom of movement shall enable any worker to engage in any occupation or profession in the Community in accordance with the principles of equal treatment as regards access to employment, working conditions and social protection in the host country.

3   The right of freedom of movement shall also imply:

—   harmonization of conditions of residence in all Member States, particularly those concerning family re-unification;

—   elimination of obstacles arising from the non-recognition of diplomas or equivalent occupational qualifications;

—   improvement of the living and working conditions of frontier workers.

Employment and Remuneration

4   Every individual shall be free to choose and engage in an occupation according to the regulations governing each occupation.

5   All employment shall be fairly remunerated.

To this end in accordance with arrangements, applying in each country:

—   workers shall be assured of an equitable wage, *ie* a wage sufficient to enable them to have a decent standard of living;

—   workers subject to terms of employment other than an open-ended full-time contract shall benefit from an equitable reference wage;

—   wages may be withheld, seized or transferred only in accordance with national law; such provisions should entail measures enabling the worker concerned to continue to enjoy the necessary means of subsistence for him or herself and his or her family.

6   Every individual must be able to have access to public place-
ment services free of charge.

Improvement of Living and Working Conditions

7   The completion of the internal market must lead to an improvement in the living and working conditions of workers in the
European Community. This process must result from an approximation of these conditions while the improvement is being
maintained as regards in particular the duration and organization of working time and forms of employment other than
open-ended contracts, such as fixed-term contracts, part-time
working, temporary work and seasonal work.

The improvement must cover, where necessary, the development of certain aspects of employment regulations such as
procedures for collective redundancies and those regarding
bankruptcies.

8   Every worker of the European Community shall have a right
to a weekly rest period and to annual paid leave, the duration
of which must be progressively harmonized in accordance with
national practices.

9   The conditions of employment of every worker of the European
Community shall be stipulated in law, a collective agreement
or a contract of employment, according to arrangements applying in each country.

Social Protection

According to the arrangements applying in each country:

10   Every worker of the European Community shall have a right to
adequate social protection and shall, whatever his status and
whatever the size of the undertaking in which he is employed,
enjoy an adequate level of social security benefits.

Persons who have been unable either to enter or re-enter the labour market and have no means of subsistence must be able to receive sufficient resources and social assistance in keeping with their particular situation.

Freedom of Association and Collective Bargaining

11 Employers and workers of the European Community shall have the right of association in order to constitute professional organizations or trade unions of their choice for the defence of their economic and social interests.

Every employer and every worker shall have the freedom to join or not to join such organizations without any personal or occupational damage being thereby suffered by him.

12 Employers or employers' organizations, on the one hand, and workers' organizations, on the other, shall have the right to negotiate and conclude collective agreements under the conditions laid down by national legislation and practice.

The dialogue between the two sides of industry at European level which must be developed may, if the parties deem it desirable, result in contractual relations in particular at inter-occupational and sectoral level.

13 The right to resort to collective action in the event of a conflict of interests shall include the right to strike, subject to the obligations arising under national regulations and collective agreements.

In order to facilitate the settlement of industrial disputes the establishment and utilization at the appropriate levels of conciliation, mediation and arbitration procedures should be encouraged in accordance with national practice.

14 The internal legal order of the Member States shall determine under which conditions and to what extent the rights provided for in Articles 11 to 13 apply to the armed forces, the police and the civil service.

Vocational Training

15   Every worker of the European Community must be able to have access to vocational training and to benefit therefrom throughout his working life. In the conditions governing access to such training there may be no discrimination of grounds of nationality.

The competent public authorities, undertakings or the two sides of industry, each within their own sphere of competence, should set up continuing and permanent training systems enabling every person to undergo retraining more especially through leave for training purposes, to improve his skills or to acquire new skills, particularly in the light of technical developments.

Equal Treatment for Men and Women

16   Equal treatment for men and women must be assured. Equal opportunities for men and women must be developed.

To this end, action should be intensified to ensure the implementation of the principle of equality between men and women as regards in particular access to employment, remuneration, working conditions, social protection, education, vocational training and career development.

Measures should also be developed enabling men and women to reconcile their occupational and family obligations.

Information, Consultation and Participation for Workers

17   Information, consultation and participation for workers must be developed along appropriate lines, taking account of the practices in force in the various Member States.

This shall apply especially in companies or groups of companies having establishments or companies in two or more Member States of the European Community.

18   Such information, consultation and participation must be imple-

mented in due time, particularly in the following cases:

— when technological changes which, from the point of view of working conditions and work organization, have major implications for the work-force, are introduced into undertakings;

— in connection with restructuring operations in undertakings or in cases of mergers having an impact on the employment of workers;

— in cases of collective redundancy procedures;

— when transfrontier workers in particular are affected by employment policies pursued by the undertaking where they are employed.

Health Protection and Safety at the Workplace

19 Every worker must enjoy satisfactory health and safety conditions in his working environment. Appropriate measures must be taken in order to achieve further harmonization of conditions in this area while maintaining the improvements made.

These measures shall take account, in particular, of the need for the training, information, consultation and balanced participation of workers as regards the risks incurred and the steps taken to eliminate or reduce them.

The provisions regarding implementation of the internal market shall help to ensure such protection.

Protection of Children and Adolescents

20 Without prejudice to such rules as may be more favourable to young people, in particular those ensuring their preparation for work through vocational training, and subject to derogations limited to certain light work, the minimum employment age must not be lower than the minimum school-leaving age and, in any case, not lower than 15 years.

21   Young people who are in gainful employment must receive equitable remuneration in accordance with national practice.

22   Appropriate measures must be taken to adjust labour regulations applicable to young workers so that their specific development and vocational training and access to employment needs are met.

   The duration of work must, in particular, be limited—without it being possible to circumvent this limitation through recourse to overtime—and night work prohibited in the case of workers under 18 years of age, save in the case of certain jobs laid down in national legislation or regulations.

23   Following the end of compulsory education, young people must be entitled to receive initial vocational training of a sufficient duration to enable them to adapt to the requirements of their future working life; for young workers such training should take place during working hours.

Elderly Persons

According to the arrangements applying in each country:

24   Every worker of the European Community must, at the time of retirement, be able to enjoy resources affording him or her a decent standard of living.

25   Any person who has reached retirement age but who is not entitled to a pension or who does not have other means of subsistence, must be entitled to sufficient resources and to medical and social assistance specifically suited to his needs.

Disabled Persons

26   All disabled persons, whatever the origin and nature of their disablement, must be entitled to additional concrete measures aimed at improving their social and professional integration.

These measures must concern, in particular, according to the capacities of the beneficiaries, vocational training, ergonomics, accessibility, mobility, means of transport and housing.

27 It is more particularly the responsibility of the Member States, in accordance with national practices, notably through legislative measures or collective agreements, to guarantee the fundamental social rights in this Charter and to implement the social measures indispensable to the smooth operation of the internal market as part of a strategy of economic and social cohesion.

28 The European Council invites the Commission to submit as soon as possible initiatives which fall within its powers, as provided for in the Treaties, with a view to the adoption of legal instruments for the effective implementation, as and when the internal market is completed of those rights which come within the Community's area of competence.

29 The Commission shall establish each year, during the last three months, a report on the application of the Charter by the Member States and by the European Community.

30 The report of the Commission shall be forwarded to the European Council, the European Parliament and the Economic and Social Committee.

References

1 Text adopted by the Heads of State or Government of 11 Member States.

Appendix II
What is the Equal Opportunities Commission?

The Equal Opportunities Commission (EOC) was set up by Act of Parliament in 1975, when Britain's two equality laws came into force: the Sex Discrimination Act and the Equal Pay Act. This process had all-party support; it began with the Conservative (Heath) government and was implemented under a Labour administration.

The Equality Agenda

Access to Justice

Issues

The laws prohibiting discrimination on grounds of sex and marital status are inadequate and unnecessarily complicated.

There are many exclusions from the protection of the equal rights laws—for example, the Armed Forces, the Church, private clubs.

Taking a case is often lengthy, costly and complicated, so that most applicants cannot take a case unaided.

The onus of proof on applicants is burdensome.

Tribunals and courts do not always have sufficient understanding of these complex and specialised laws to ensure their consistent application.

Remedies are inadequate and enforcement of awards is difficult and costly. Some successful applicants never receive the full amount of their award.

Victimisation provisions are inadequate and women are fearful of taking their cases to law.

In indirect discrimination claims, compensation cannot be awarded where the discrimination is unintentional.

The definition of indirect discrimination is too narrow.

The law on equal pay for work of equal value is complicated and parts are still unclear. A successful outcome only benefits that individual applicant and does not extend to others in the same employment. Taking equal pay claims is extremely expensive and long delays are onerous on an individual.

Causes

Our equality laws are contained in two separate Acts rather than a single one. It is sometimes unclear which Act applies, and some provisions in the two Acts are inconsistent. This has led to confusion and added to the costs of cases.

Taking discrimination and equal pay cases in the industrial tribunals has proved far more difficult than anticipated because of the complexity of the laws and the formality of the process.

The law is now contained in a bewildering number of sources, brought together by means of a piecemeal process.

Since the domestic laws were introduced a variety of European laws and directives have come into play. Consequently there is no single comprehensive statement of the law.

Recommendations

The unduly complex statutory framework of the sex discrimination and the equal pay laws should be replaced by a single statute, the Equal Treatment Act, consolidating existing law and taking account of European Community law. The associated regulations should be written clearly and concisely.

The revised legislation should encompass the full range of activities of the State. The existing exemptions are no longer appropriate and should be repealed.

Tribunal and Court procedures should be reviewed and simplified. Once the applicant proves less favourable treatment consistent with sex or marital status has occurred, the burden of proof should be on the respondent to prove discrimination did not occur.

Specialised training should be given to all members of Industrial Tribunals and the Employment Appeal Tribunal.

More women members should be recruited.

Compensation in successful sex discrimination cases is too low. There should be a basic minimum award of £500 (plus a compensatory award). There should be no artificial ceilings to awards; individuals should be compensated for all of their loss.

Tribunals should have the same power to order reinstatement in cases of sex discrimination in dismissal as they have in unfair dismissal cases.

The redress for victimisation is ineffective. The Act should be amended to encompass anyone who attempts to prevent justice being done. In addition to any compensatory award there should be a basic minimum award of £1000 in victimisation cases.

The definition of indirect discrimination should be expanded and clarified.

Compensation should be awarded for both intentional and unintentional indirect discrimination.

In equal pay and equal value claims:

- The law on equal value should be clarified and the procedures simplified.
- More independent experts should be appointed and strict time limits imposed for their reports.
- When an applicant succeeds, all employees in the same employment who do the same or broadly similar work should

be entitled to the same award including back pay.

Industrial Tribunals (or similar body) should have jurisdiction to hear claims of discrimination in the terms of collective agreements brought by any interested party, including the Equal Opportunities Commission.

Equal Rights at Work

Issues

Although the Sex Discrimination and Equal Pay Acts were in place in 1975, many people still miss out on equal treatment at work.

They include—

Pregnant women: Despite the EOC establishing that dismissal on the grounds of pregnancy may be unlawful, women are still being dismissed when they become pregnant.

Nearly half of those women, who become pregnant while in employment, are not eligible for maternity leave. They have no automatic right to maternity benefits to return to their jobs.

Part-time employees: There are currently 5.4 million part-time employees in Britain and 83% of them are women. Many who have worked less than five years for the same employer are excluded from employment protection rights including unfair dismissal. Part-timers may receive, pro rata, lower rates of pay than full-timers. When business is bad, part-timers are often the first to have their pay cut, their hours reduced or to be selected for redundancy. Even when they have worked for an employer for many years, their status is often low and they are unlikely to be promoted or offered training. Many part-timers do not have access to pensions, holiday pay or performance pay.

People who want to do jobs that are seen as 'women's work' or 'men's work' face unnecessary obstacles to their choice: For instance, men wanting to look after the elderly or children can have a hard time getting a job and are often treated with suspicion. Equally, women may be prevented from doing work considered dirty or physically demanding. If they seek a job which needs technical or mechanical knowledge, or want to develop management or leadership skills, they can find it difficult to get training, let alone the chance of promotion.

People on the receiving end of sexual harassment: This is not a new problem and it is not a joke. It is objectionable and offensive behaviour which causes distress, strain and ill-health. It prevents people from doing their jobs properly.

Black and ethnic minority women: They may have even more limited choices, and can face a double dose of discrimination in every aspect of their working life.

Women serving in the armed forces: The 18,600 women currently serving in the Army, Navy and Air Force have limited rights to maternity leave and to return to work. As service in the armed forces is not covered by the Sex Discrimination Act they cannot challenge this in an Industrial Tribunal.

Causes

Outmoded attitudes and assumptions still prevail. All too often employers focus on the sex of the job-holder rather than looking at the person's aspirations and their ability to do the job. Low expectations may especially affect black and ethnic minority women.

Half of the women who become pregnant at work are not eligible for paid maternity leave and the right to return to their jobs. Hence many women are forced to leave their jobs, often at a crucial time in their careers. A recent EOC report on the million women in the NHS shows that many skilled nurses returning from child-bearing have their talents and experience wasted and their career prospects cut short by having to work in lower grades and without the responsibilities given to full-timers.

Sexual harassment is often not taken seriously by management. People who have experience harassment are reluctant to make complaints for fear of losing their jobs, or damaging their chance of promotion.

Recommendations

An extension of full maternity rights to all pregnant women in employment.

A change in the law removing the restrictions of many part-timers from enjoying the benefits of employment protection rights.

Better measures to tackle sexual harassment need to be incorporated into the Sex Discrimination Act.

Employers should provide flexible working hours, recognise and reward skills and give access to the training needed for advancement. Unions should take steps to involve part-timers in setting the bargaining agenda.

Equal Pay

Issues

Women today still only earn 78% of men's hourly earnings and even less when weekly earnings are involved.

The labour market is still largely split into men's jobs and women's jobs. Women's jobs are often low paid and under-valued. For instance, average weekly earnings for women manual workers in hair-dressing are £110.30 as against the national average of £221.20 for manual workers (10% of women in hairdressing earn less than £75.90 a week). Average weekly earnings for women manual workers in the hotel and catering industry are £126.20 (10% of women earn less than £83.50).

Some employers rely on low-pay for competitive advantage.

Low-pay means lower living standards, poor housing and poverty in old age.

Causes

Pay in equalities are deeply rooted. Special rates of pay for women doing the same job as men became illegal in 1975. Many jobs however, have traditionally been assigned to one sex or the other, so even today women's work continues to receive lower pay.

Overtime payments, bonuses and allowances make a big difference to take-home pay, but women may not be eligible for such payments, or may receive them at a lower rate.

Payment systems themselves may be discriminatory.

Part-timers have limited pay and career prospects. (There are 4.5 million part-time women workers in Britain—83% of the part-time workforce.)

Discriminatory pay practices have been sustained by collective agreements.

People lack knowledge of their rights under UK Equal Value law and European law. The legislation is complicated and parts are still unclear even after seven years of operation. It relies on the individual to take action but an individual needs legal and financial support and also almost superhuman determination and a thick skin

Delays discourage genuine applicants. On average, it is 7 months from the time a complaint is first filed to the first tribunal hearing. Independent experts take an average of 12 months to complete their reports. A case going to Employment Appeal Tribunal takes on average another one-and-a-half years. It is not unusual for a case to take three or four years.

Recommendations

The Equal Value legislation needs to be more sharply defined and made more effective.

The Equal Opportunities Commission is calling for changes in the Tribunal process to—

— Cut delays on individual cases.

— Provide training for Tribunal members.

— Tackle discriminatory practices in employers' rules and terms and in collective agreements.

— Extend awards of a successful applicant to employees doing the same or similar work.

If justice is to be seen to be done, the law itself must be simplified and the separate confusing treatment in the two existing Acts replaced with a simpler, fairer Equal Treatment Act.

A Code of Practice, to guide both employers and trade unions on avoiding sex discrimination in pay, is necessary.

Initiatives must be taken to increase awareness of employees of their rights under British and European Community law.

We support the European Commission's intention to adopt a memorandum on equal pay for equal value and provide guidance on job evaluation.

Pay and benefits should be the same or pro rata for part-timers and full-timers.

Low pay has a particular impact on women, many of whom are in a vulnerable position and are among those least assisted by law or collective bargaining, *eg* homeworkers.

The Equal Opportunities Commission has argued in the past that wage protection should be extended to groups of low paid workers and is therefore, currently considering the likely impact of a national minimum wage on the gender gap in pay.

The Equal Opportunities Commission would like to see the party in government get together a package of measure that will make a real impact on this matter.

Education and Training

Issues

Compared with men, women end up in a more limited range of lower paid occupations with less training provision, fewer career prospects and less job satisfaction. This represents a waste of talent which the country cannot afford. It happens in spite of the fact that girls achieve more GCSE passes than boys, and achieve higher grades. They have almost caught up at A level too. In Scotland, girls already do better than boys in 'Highers' as well as 'Standard' grades, and more graduates are women. Yet Scottish women occupy the same narrow range of occupations.

Gender segregation starts at school. Research shows that many girls' choices of subjects are still affected by a pressure form society to conform with roles that are thought to be 'suitable' for them.

This starts girls off on separate tramlines from boys, from which they find it difficult to escape later on. The effects carry on into their training and career opportunities throughout their lives. There may be especially low expectations of black and ethnic minority girls.

Too often girls leave school with unjustifiably limited ambitions; not surprising in view of the role models in the school—women are 79% of primary school teachers but only 46% head teachers; they are 47% of secondary school teachers but only 17% of head teachers.

In further and higher education, the gender segregation in subjects studied intensifies. Only 11% of engineering undergraduates are women, and women are still grossly under-represented in physics and mathematics.

Young women not in full-time education are disadvantaged in training:

— One in three men compared with one in five women in employment receive training.

— The training received by women tends to be shorter in duration.

— Within manufacturing occupations, young men are two to

three time more likely to be receiving training than young women.

— Less than a third of those on day/block release are girls.

— On the publicly funded Youth Training Programme, women are streamed into traditionally female areas of training— mainly clerical and administrative work.

Female adult employees also receive less training than their male counterparts:

— Women part-time employees are less likely to receive training than women full-timers or men. (43% of all women workers are part-timers).

— Training tends to be grade-related and women receive less because they are in lower occupational grades.

— Women are disproportionately concentrated in small establishments which are less likely to provide training.

— At graduate level, men are more likely to go into industries and occupations with opportunities for training.

— Training provision for women who wish to return to employment after a career break is inadequate to their needs.

Causes

There is still strong pressure from society for girls to conform to stereotyped expectations. There is an implied series of messages that say 'Don't be too competitive, don't appear too bright, especially in boys' subjects' and there is a general assumption that girls will be less able at scientific, mathematical and technical subjects. This is not borne out by reality—for instance, although there are fewer girls attempting GCSEs in physics and technology, those who do, achieve better results than the boys.

The National Curriculum will reduce subject segregation up to the age of 16 but is unlikely to affect what happens afterwards unless all subjects are made appealing to both girls and boys. Post-16, girls predominate in English, modern languages, creative arts and commercial, domestic subjects. Boys predominate in physics, chemistry, mathematics and technology. this affects entry patterns to further/ higher education and to types of jobs. It effectively cuts off girls from many excellent career opportunities in an increasingly technological society. Curriculum patterns within Scottish schools reflect a similar situation to that in England and Wales.

The low status of traditionally female jobs puts women at a disadvantage in terms of promotion and training.

The potential of women re-entering the job market after child-rearing is insufficiently recognised. The provision of training is also unsuited to their requirements. Most training is geared to the continuous work pattern of men's lives.

Recommendations

A coherent, national term training strategy, recognising the benefits of equal opportunities and involving partnerships between government, employers, unions, trainers and trainees, with clear qualitative and quantitative targets and realistic funding from central government.

Training for teachers, governors and managers of schools and colleges to combat gender stereotyping.

Careers counselling free from sexual and cultural bias.

Mandatory grants for part-time degree courses for mature students.

Training provision which fits in with part-time hours and family commitments.

Help with costs and availability of quality child care for trainees, together with the costs of training and travel.

A training system which is sufficiently flexible to allow career change and retraining at different points in the working lifetime, so that choices made at the age of 16 are not irrevocable.

More widespread understanding and use of positive action initiatives providing career structure and training opportunities in jobs at all levels.

Family Policy and Child Care

Issues

Women with young children make a significant contribution to the workforce and to the output of the nation. Affordable child care is the single item that figures most in what mothers say they need. Yet they receive almost no help with this from the State. Private nurseries, though growing in number, are beyond the purses of most women.

Forty per cent of all women with a youngest child under school-age work either full-time or part-time. There are 1.2 million of them and research shows that a further half-million mothers of young children would work in they could find affordable alternative child care.

Compared with our European partners, UK public provision for children below school-age and for out-of-school care is meagre in the extreme. Government responsibility for child care provision under the Children Act is currently limited to children 'in need' up to the age of 8.

Maternity/paternity provision is inadequate. Approximately 45% of women in the UK have no legal right to maternity leave. Paternity leave is almost unknown and rarely in option for fathers in Britain. Income replacement during maternity leave is less than in any other European Community country.

Rights to employment leave for family-care purposes are inadequate.

Causes

Society had changed as more women with young children work yet no government has addressed the consequences. Statutory rights and individual employment contracts do not fully meet the needs of working parents—for instance, in areas like parental or paternity leave and time off for family reasons.

Outdated attitudes and beliefs (men breadwinners: women home-makers) linger on in the minds of people who have influence and power to make changes in society, and inhibit progress. Recent studies demonstrate, for instance, that good early years' experiences outside the home do not harm but, on the contrary, actually help children's development, their communication skills, their confidence and their health.

Caring for children and dependent adults has traditionally been seen as women's work, paid badly or not at all. Assumptions about women's economic dependency continue to influence policy (for instance, the low level of State-financed income replacement during maternity leave).

Government's approach to family policies is limited by the view that the family should function as a private unit with minimal involvement or support from public authorities.

Recommendations

Government commitment to develop child care services with the ultimate aim of making accessible a place in an appropriate child care setting for every child whose parent(s) want it.

Overall responsibility for under-5s child care services to be co-ordinated under one government department with a National Development Agency to initiate:

— A national framework for the development of a variety of child care services in every area for young children and their families.

— A new approach to funding child care based on a three-way split between government/employers/parents.

— A resource for training, to professionalise child-caring with a view to maintaining quality of care in the face of an increase in demand.

— The establishment of minimum standards for child care

which would be binding on local authorities in their registering and inspecting capacity.

The progressive removal from the tax and benefit systems of the remaining measure which perpetuate the concept of women's economic dependency, and their replacement with individual rights.

A government-led debate about how to manage more equitably the caring responsibilities in our society. As national employment needs and women's expectations change and the size of the elderly population grows, the invisible unpaid system of care traditionally provided by women may no longer be available to meet the need.

Government action to support and facilitate a greater role for men as carers, including statutory rights to take up paternity or parental leave and time off for family reasons.

Employers and trade union negotiators to develop a range of flexible family-friendly policies and working arrangements.

More adequate financial recognition to all informal carers to recognise the important role they play in the community care.

State Pensions

Issues

Currently, men still have to wait until 65, five years longer than women, to get their pensions. The Government's recent commitment to equalisation of the pension ages after consultation about the options is very welcome.

Because of the different pensions ages, men pay contributions for 44 years while women pay only for 39 years, before qualifying for a full basic pension.

There is little choice for either sex about when they want to retire and receive a pension.

Many men and women do not now retire at 65 and 60. The current state pension ages therefore no longer match people's needs.

Women on average do less well than men under the State Earnings Related Pension Scheme (SERPS). Yet more women than men rely on SERPS to top up their basic pension.

The use of pension ages to limit eligibility for other social security benefits cuts off women five years before men from claiming some benefits—such as Severe Disablement Allowance or Invalid Care Allowance.

Pensions do not keep up with general improvements in the standard of living. The very old, predominantly women, therefore manage on the lowest pensions.

Causes

The different pension ages arose from special political considerations during the Second World War, and have remained unchanged ever since.

Women's pay is on average lower than men's, which depresses their SERPS entitlement as this is calculated on average lifetime earnings to depress their SERPS entitlement further.

Many elderly women who now rely on means-tested benefits were encouraged to rely on their husbands to provide an income for their old age, and so did not acquire any individual pension rights.

The link between State pensions and increases in average earnings has been abandoned.

Recommendations

The government should now act speedily on its commitment to equalise State pension ages and should do in a way which leaves most people better, not worse off.

The European Commission's draft proposal for a further Directive on equal treatment in social security should be supported. This in itself would require equal pension ages.

The National Insurance contributions system should be equalised, and the use of discriminatory pension ages as the cut-off point for claiming other benefits should be abandoned.

Emphasis should be placed on every individual having their own entitlement, so that fewer and fewer women depend on their husbands' benefits, which are vulnerable in the event of divorce or widowhood.

SERPS entitlement should be based, as originally, on the best twenty years of earnings and not on average lifetime earnings, a system which disadvantages women.

Priority should be given to improving the level of the basic State pension.

Occupational Pensions

Issues

On 17 May 1990 the European Court of Justice decided that, for the purposes of European law, occupational pensions are pay. This means that in future occupational pension schemes must treat women and men equally.

It is not yet clear, however, whether this applies to all pensions paid after the date of the judgment, or only to rights acquired in pension schemes from that date.

The case in question, Barber v Guardian Royal Exchange, was essentially about pension ages. It is also not yet clear whether, or how, certain other pensions arrangements (*eg* widower's pensions) need to be equalised.

In order to introduce genuine equality, wide-ranging changes are needed in occupational pension schemes and there is a need for new 'partnership' arrangements (between the State and private providers) for schemes contracted out of State Earnings Related Pension Scheme (SERPS).

Meanwhile, many women who are members of schemes are being told by their employer that their pension age will be raised from 60 to 65—before it has been established whether or not this procedure is lawful.

Many other women still do not have access to their company pension scheme at all—usually because they work part-time.

Women members of schemes often lose out of their pension entitlement, because they have breaks in paid employment due to caring responsibilities in the home.

Causes

The first cause is the length of time it has taken for any UK government to 'grasp the nettle' on equal treatment in relation to pensions in general, and the State pension age in particular.

Another cause now is genuine uncertainty about what the law requires (see previous column).

Contracting-out requirements for occupational pension schemes make it extremely difficult at present to achieve equal treatment, because they are based on the unequal State pension ages.

The use made of separate-sex actuarial tables often leads to unequal treatment of women and men in pensions.

Many women are not in a position to take care of their occupational pension rights during breaks in employment because of caring responsibilities.

Recommendations

All interested parties should welcome the government's recent commitment to equalise the State pension ages and join with the EOC in pressing for a swift decision about when and how to do it.

The 'partnership' arrangements between the State and private schemes should be revised as soon as possible, so as to facilitate equal treatment.

New proposals should be formulated by government to secure the pension rights, at least to an equalised guarantee minimum, of people taking time off work for caring responsibilities.

Employers should be required to encourage those returning from career breaks to 'buy back', if it all possible, full pension rights for years spent away from paid work.

The exception in the Sex Discrimination Act (s.45) which allows the use of separate-sex actuarial tables to result, for example, in additional voluntary contributions costing women more than men, should be repealed.

Part-time employees should be given the right to join occupational pension schemes.

More information should be made available about the relative advantages and disadvantages of the various pension options and arrangements, for people with different working life patterns.